Lies Jane Austen Told Me
Published by EAB Publishing (2015)
Copyright EAB Publishing (2015)

Text copyright Julie Rowse

Cover photo used with permission
Copyright Ashley Crawford Photography

Cover and chapter title font: Pea Steele by
kevinandamanda.com/fonts

Scripture quotations taken from the New English Bible,
copyright © Cambridge University Press and Oxford
University Press 1961, 1970. All rights reserved.

ISBN 10: 0692512489
ISBN 13: 978-0692512487

# Filmography

*Pretty in Pink,* 1986. Dir. Howard Deutch, Written by John Hughes.
Preppy boy pursues girl from wrong side of the Trax. Girl's male best friend actually in love with her.

*Some Kind of Wonderful,* 1987. Dir. Howard Deutch, Written by John Hughes
Boy thinks he is in love with the school's most popular girl, only to realize he's in love with his tomboy BFF.

*Say Anything,* 1989. Dir. and written by Cameron Crowe
Uber-sensitive boy unsure of his post-high school plans falls in love with scientifically-minded girl who's been accepted to Oxford.

*Singles,* 1992. Dir. and written by Cameron Crowe
Several twenty-something couples navigate relationships against grungy Seattle landscape.

# Bibliography—All by Jane Austen

*Persuasion*--Old maid pines eight years for the love of her life to return to her.

*Pride and Prejudice*--Man of privilege deigns to fall in love with woman of a lower class.

*Northanger Abbey*--Girl with a penchant for the dramatic gets to marry man of her dreams despite many obstacles.

*Sense and Sensibility*--Two sisters judge each other's romantic choices.

*Emma*--Girl spends her life hooking up all of her friends and realizes in the process she has fallen in love.

Love is a smoke made with the fume of sighs,
Being purged, a fire sparkling in lovers' eyes,
Being vexed, a sea nourished with lovers' tears.
What is it else?
A madness most discreet,
A choking gall and a preserving sweet.

*--Romeo and Juliet*
William Shakespeare

## Key Characters

*Pretty in Pink*
Duckie Dale--Shamelessly in love with his best friend Andie.
Andie--Loves vintage clothes and being courted by the upper class.
Blaine--Loves Andie. Most of the time.

*Some Kind of Wonderful*
Keith--Lusts for Amanda Jones. Loves his BFF Watts.
Amanda Jones--Popular girl at school, dating a cretin. Agrees to one date with Keith as payback for said cretin's infidelity.
Watts--Lusts for her drums. Loves her BFF Keith.

*Say Anything*
Diane Court--Smart but socially stunted girl unaware of her beauty and appeal. Gives horrible breakup gifts.
Lloyd Dobler--Quite aware of Diane's beauty and appeal. Writes beautiful post-coital letters, which serve as catalysts for horrible breakup gifts.

*Singles*
Steve Dunn--Hopeless romantic who believes unlocking a car door in a pre-power lock age is an unmistakable sign of compatibility.
Linda Powell--Pragmatic environmentalist who is afraid of men loving her.
Cliff Poncier--Lead singer of a grunge band with an affinity for busty women. Also good at leading on less-busty women.
Janet Livermore--Barista in love with Cliff, who longs for someone to say "bless you" when she sneezes.

Wickham (*Pride and Prejudice*)--Elizabeth Bennet's first suitor. Later revealed to not be a good match for her.

Bingley (*Pride and Prejudice*)--Kind and decent wealthy man in love with Elizabeth Bennet's older sister Jane.

Knightley (*Emma*)--Wise friend to Emma, he endures her shenanigans until she realizes he loves her.

Tilney (*Northanger Abbey*)--Handsome and flirtatious man who eventually allows himself to fall in love with Catherine Morland.

Willoughby (*Sense and Sensibility*)--Incredibly handsome, Marianne quickly falls in love with him only to realize he is not as genuine as she initially thought.

Col. Brandon (*Sense and Sensibility*)--Not as handsome or young as Willoughby, but much more trustworthy.

Author's Note:

In an effort to protect the privacy of the people in my life, the following accommodations have been made:

All names of my suitors have been changed to a Jane Austen character name.

Names of women related to my suitors have been changed to protect their identity.

Some locations have been changed.

# Lies Jane Austen Told Me

by Julie L. Rowse

My very first journal.

# Lies Jane Austen Told Me

I can still remember the first time I wanted to get married.

Kyle, a brown-haired, freckle-faced gent, lived three houses away, and we often walked to school together.

On this day, the day I planned to marry him, we sat in high-backed vinyl chairs, decorated in the brown and mustard floral color scheme of the 1970s, at my mother's kitchen table while munching on sandwiches. Kyle and I were perfect for each other—we both loved *Star Wars* and we were both Mormon. Those two characteristics served as deal breakers. Match made in heaven. I had the dress, I had the boy, and as soon as we finished our peanut butter sandwiches, we were going to take a bus to Salt Lake City and marry.

In my youthful innocence, I overlooked four key details.

First, we lived in California, and Salt Lake City was a long way away.

Second, we had no money.

Third, the dress I had was a powder blue and sunflower yellow Holly Hobbie Calico number, and to marry in Mormon temples, brides wear white.

Fourth, I was five years old.

The finer details of that day are a bit hazy (such as

Kyle's reaction to our plan), but this much is clear: at five years old, I knew I wanted to be married, and I wanted to be married to a boy. A Mormon boy.

I grew up in a traditional Mormon household: my dad worked and my mom stayed home. She was an incredible mother. I completely took for granted that if I was sick at school, she would pick me up 20 minutes later, or if I left my lunch on the counter, it would be in my hands by noon. My dad was an officer in the Air Force, and though he eschewed the distant rules-with-an-iron-fist military dad stereotype, the surest way to incur his wrath was to disrespect my mom. He refused to tolerate it. My parents went on dates nearly every Friday night, and to this day, they still hold hands when they walk in public.

It's cute. And disgusting.

Their relationship is what I always wanted, and frankly, what I expected was my birthright. They raised me, my two sisters, and my brother as faithful members of The Church of Jesus Christ of Latter-Day Saints (LDS, or familiarly, Mormon). I grew up singing songs like "Families Can Be Together Forever" and "When I Grow Up, I Want To Be A Mother." While the first song reflects LDS doctrine and is earnest and heartfelt, the second song has cringe-worthy lyrics, explaining a young girl's excitement and anticipation at having up to six children under her God-given maternal care.

I've spent most of the past two decades separating what is cultural about my faith from what is doctrinal. I'm at a point now where I believe gender roles, like the ones reflected in those lyrics, are cultural and not doctrinal. I have often wondered if my own mother ever felt a little bit "less than" for only having four kids, instead of the seemingly requisite seven or eight that was common in LDS families in the 1970s. But for all the struggle I have with cultural elements of LDS, the good it brings to my life really does outweigh the more challenging aspects of being a single member of such a family-centered church. Without going into a lengthy discussion, my faith gives me peace and perspective. It gives me a built-in family no matter where I go. It is part of the glue that holds my real family together.

At the same time, however, being Mormon is not the toothy Donny and Marie Prozac-induced giddiness so often portrayed in the church's commercials. Our family fought and cried as often as we played together and laughed. Marriage is the ultimate goal of many Mormons. In all the youth lessons and activities I attended, and even in religion classes at Brigham Young University, living my life as a single woman was never even floated to me as a possibility. Not once. It was assumed that at least one person on this planet would find me tolerable for time and all eternity. So as an adult, despite the Christian directive to accept and love all, the church culture sometimes looks at me—a single and childless woman in her 40s—and thinks "What a failure. What did she do wrong?"

At my last Sunday service before going to BYU as a sparkling 18-year-old, the elder stateswomen of the ward pulled me aside. Surrounded by a fog of patchouli and gardenia and no visible escape route, I watched as three 60-year-old women offered advice and predictions.

"Never say no to a date!"

"Be sure to go to concerts with the boys—the classical music there is wonderfully romantic!"

"Set up lots of group dates with your roommates. It is so much fun!"

Their voices and painted-on eyebrows moved higher and higher, as with twinkles in their eyes they warned, "You'll be engaged by Christmas, just watch!"

I shyly demurred; I still hadn't broken up with my non-Mormon high school boyfriend who was going to school in Colorado. Yet part of me hoped these women were right. It was not uncommon for couples at BYU to meet in September, be engaged by December, and marry in April. Heck, it wasn't uncommon for couples at BYU to meet on Labor Day, be engaged by Halloween, and marry at Thanksgiving. I saw it happen every semester. A girl would meet the "perfect" return missionary (a 21-year-old man who had sacrificed two years of his life to spread the gospel often in places like Latvia or Madagascar, but just as often in places like Toledo or Boise) and date him daily. These dates included free concerts at the Harris Fine Arts Center, ice cream at the BYU Creamery, movies—with all questionable language, nudity, and excessive violence removed—at the on-campus theater, study sessions at the library, and dances. Always there were dances.

After about a month of daily dates, these couples have a conversation. They decide it's time to pray about whether they should pursue a relationship that will lead to marriage. With all of my girlfriends at BYU, that answer was never "no." So every semester, I would take part in the most dreaded of college rituals: the Candle Ceremony. This sorority-style ritual usually occurred within a day of an official engagement; it was a cloak and dagger way of revealing which girl's entire existence was validated with a diamond. These girls were chosen and anointed as bastions of femininity and worthiness. They would not spend a lifetime looking for ways to justify their existence, for they were fulfilling their purpose in life: to be a wife and a mother.

I would sit in a circle of 15 or 20 girls, mentally flipping through my head who each girl was dating. A lit candle was passed from girl to girl, and when the betrothed received the candle, she would extinguish it, signaling her foray into Married Life. I always held my breath when a roommate held the candle. I loved my roommates, and I didn't want to lose any of them to a man. When the candle reached me, I was tempted to blow it out, signaling that I was actually The Desired One, but I always chickened out. As I passed the candle to the next girl, I imagined the candle to be a birthday candle, mentally blowing it out and wishing that soon I would be the subject of a Candlelight Ceremony.

Part of the quick courtship/engagement rationale is the LDS belief in chastity before marriage. No sex or sex-like shenanigans are allowed until after the wedding. For hormonal young LDS couples, this means relatively short courtships. But marrying young isn't just about

5

sex. It's a cultural imperative. It's what's been done for generations. Though it did not work out, I was engaged at 20 after six months of dating. One of my sisters married at 19. My other sister, after completing her Associate's Degree at a local community college, said, "I want to get married, so I'm going to go to BYU." Eighteen months later, she was married. She was 21. So it really was difficult to not feel like a complete failure when I attended her wedding, single, the day after I turned 25.

Apparently, the elder stateswomen of my ward in Montana needed to specify by which Christmas I would be snatched up, because by the time three BYU Christmases had passed, without any dating success in Mormon Mecca, I wasn't engaged to the LDS dream I'd been raised to believe was rightfully mine. And I wasn't sure it was ever going to happen. That was over 20 years ago, and while I am proud of my career, my volunteer work, this life that I've had to create for myself to compensate for not wiving and mothering, I struggle at times with a belief that my life will only be considered valuable once a man decides I am good enough to marry. My career is a consolation prize, second place to what I really should have won.

That said, as I get older and my hopeful romanticism wanes, I realize my church is not solely responsible for my warped view of why it sucks to be single. Something about an episode of How I Met Your Mother reminded me that I also blame other people for making me feel like my single life is not worthwhile.

In the episode, Ted has long been searching for his

one and only, and after yet another friend announces his marriage, and other friends announce a pregnancy, Ted tells his ex-girlfriend Robin that over the years, he has slowly stopped believing in ever finding his destined soul mate.

Robin tells Ted that he needs to believe again, but not in destiny. Instead, she reminds him that like many things in life, timing is the ultimate arbiter of mating. It's also the key element of soul-mate searching that no one can control.

Like a flash, I realized my parents didn't deserve all the blame for my unrealistic expectations of relationships, and neither did my church. No, three people deserve to share that burden.

John Hughes, Cameron Crowe, and Jane Austen.

I was 13 years old when I first experienced the fake love of a John Hughes movie. One John Hughes movie led to another, which was a gateway to Cameron Crowe's work, and by the time I was in college, I spent an entire semester freebasing Jane Austen. Working in tandem at different points in my life, their art influenced me to believe things I should not have. They perpetuated outdated and irrational myths about how love and relationships work. Their genealogy goes back to Shakespeare, and the Academy is split on whether he actually wrote his own plays anyway, so really, in the world of entertainment, no one can be trusted.

Chuck Klosterman spends the entire first chapter of *Sex, Drugs, and Cocoa Puffs* ranting about how Lloyd Dobler, the attentive, adorable boyfriend in Cameron

Crowe's *Say Anything*, completely ruined dating for all men because of something he calls "the prospect of fake love." For Klosterman, fake love is the result of various popular culture icons, from Coldplay to Journey, from Bridget Jones to the Huxtables. These popular culture texts tell me that someone will "fix me," that a man will "faithfully" be mine, that he will like me "just as I am," and eventually marry me, breed with me, and live in a trendy brownstone in New York City.

However, these are all lies that can be traced back to the collective works of Jane Austen, including the following:

**I would marry my best friend.** This was my hemlock, because my best friends were always guys, and many of those friendships began because I had uber-crushes on them. Hughes and Crowe especially convinced me that if I held out long enough, my best guy friend du jour would, in a flashy epiphany, realize how much he loved me. Silly rabbit, flashy epiphanies are what screenwriters create. And while plenty of people claim to marry their best friends—and I'm jealous happy for them—so far, for me, it is a myth.

**If my best friend was just a bit too quirky for me to marry, a dashing man outside my social circle would seek me out for my own quirkiness and marry me.** Between my failing memory and my meticulous journals, I cannot recall a dashing man outside my social circle ever seeking me out. Most of the time, if a dashing man outside my social circle talked to me, it was for one of three reasons: he needed help with homework; he needed a ride somewhere; he wanted a date with one of my thin and beautiful girlfriends. Dashing men are fiction. Dashing men do not see past the glasses, the sarcasm, and the 20 extra pounds. Dashing men stick to gorgeous women.

**Being smart is totally okay and not at all intimidating.** I once dated a guy who loved to play trivia games. I had to purposely "throw" games so he wouldn't be mad at me. I was way smarter than him and knew tons more useless information, but I purposely lost every time we played a trivia game because he did not like losing to a girl. Similarly, one guy I was engaged to told me girls didn't need to go to college. I don't know if it's rampant male insecurity or if I am unwittingly condescending, but my intelligence has never led me to the affections of a man. If anything, my intelligence has been a major roadblock to securing a man.

**If I fight nonstop with a guy, we will end up getting married.** Nope. If I fight nonstop with a guy, it usually means that we don't agree politically or that he thinks Batman is a superhero. Both of these opinions create impossible chasms to bridge. He usually doesn't find my passion endearing, and I usually don't find his boorishness hot. If we're fighting, we will not reach a point in the fight where, mid-scream, we start kissing. We may, however, reach a point where I throw something at him and storm out of the room.

**I will get married.** And this is where that episode of *How I Met Your Mother* served as a catalyst for this epiphany. I suppose if you want to be technical, neither Hughes nor Crowe ended their films with a wedding. Though for most girls, it's implied that Samantha Baker becomes Mrs. Jake Ryan, Watts becomes Mrs. Keith Nelson, and Janet Livermore becomes Mrs. Cliff Poncier. And every single Jane Austen book ends with a wedding. The timing is always perfect, because the story has to end eventually. So while the movies might avoid the marriage issue, the books certainly don't. While my parents and my church never prepared me for a life lived utterly alone, neither did the movies I watched or the books I read.

I've attended many, many weddings. I'm now in the phase of life where I am attending weddings of former students. Why didn't John Hughes make that movie? Samantha Baker grows up, doesn't marry Jake Ryan, teaches at a high school, and goes to all of her former students' weddings. Why not make that movie? Or write that book? Because no one would see that movie or read that book.

It's too damn depressing.

# I Am Duckie.

When I was 13, my youth group advisor took a giggly group of 12 and 13 year old girls to see *Pretty in Pink*. That was my first exposure to the mythic class conflict romance that made me believe there was a Blaine out there somewhere who didn't care that I was a little insecure about my looks or my middle-class economic status. It was also my first exposure to a John Hughes film, and it came at a time when I was particularly impressionable. Not just because I was 13 and all 13-year-olds are impressionable, but because I was a complete and total misfit, wondering if a boy who wasn't my friend would ever like me.

We lived in Alabama at the time, and one rule in our house was no makeup until 14. This immediately set me up as a freak within my youth group, as most Southern Belles first visited the Clinique counter at 10 years old. But while the girls at church ostracized me for my lack of femininity, the boys at church embraced me for it. Kevin, Tyler, Brian, Marc, and Matt talked to me, hung out with me at church activities and at school, made me feel special. They wanted me on their team when we played any type of trivia game. In the days before text messaging and smart phones, they wrote me notes and shoved them in my hand in the junior high school hallways. By spring, Marc and I formed a deep enough connection that he made the ultimate declaration of 13-year-old love: he told me we had a song. "Something About You" by the one hit wonder Level 42 apparently expressed perfectly how Marc felt about me.

Those ten months in Alabama should have prepared me for a lifetime of allowing myself to be chased and courted and treasured. As much of a tomboy I was to them with my no makeup-wearing and constant sports-talking ways, they flirted with me incessantly. And I loved it.

When I walked out of *Pretty in Pink,* I knew I had witnessed my future. Marc had already declared his love for me; it was just a matter of time before we'd be kissing at prom. But two months later, he moved to Texas, I moved to Nebraska, and we lost touch in a pre-Facebook era. In the years since, I've noticed that Andie and I had so much in common. We were both misfits. We were both smart. We were both detached yet hopeful. We both had a male best friend, and though Duckie doesn't tell Andie right away that he loves her, I'm pretty sure she knew, and rather than break his heart, she maintained the friendship as best she could. Here is the major problem with my connection though: I am not Andie. I am Duckie.

Several years ago, I was out with a friend and told her about my idea for this book. When I told her that I am Duckie, her face fell and her head tilted from "interested" to "pity." It was a head tilt I'd seen dozens of times. When I try to make sense of why I am single, the default response from friends and family is to negate any criticism I levy against myself.

"You are not!" she insisted.

"Yes I am, at least with one of my relationships. Maybe not all of them, but definitely one of them," I replied. But it got me thinking: is being like Duckie really a bad thing? Here is what I see when I watch *Pretty in Pink*:

**Duckie always makes Andie laugh.** This is an excellent quality in a significant other. There's enough drama in relationships, and if at least one person involved can't find a way to laugh, then the relationship is doomed. Did Blaine ever make Andie laugh? No. Blaine might have been hot, but if John Hughes had bothered to make *Pretty in Pink 2: Blaine and Andie After Ten Years of Marriage*, I'm pretty sure Blaine would be cheating and Andie would be an alcoholic. Laughter can prevent this type of tragedy in relationships.

**Duckie always defends Andie.** Even when the Evil Stef insinuates that Andie is a tramp, Duckie supports her. He is loyal, possibly to a fault. Was Blaine? Not even close. Blaine doesn't answer the phone when Andie calls, and she has to confront him at school. She screams in his face, demanding an answer for why he is avoiding her. She didn't have to do that with Duckie. And wouldn't you want someone who is always on your side?

**Duckie shows up even after they fight.** Andie goes to prom by herself, probably wishing she and Duckie were on speaking terms. She realizes how humiliating it would actually be to walk through the doors--you can see her decide to turn around and leave. But there's Duckie. Dressed for prom, ready for anything, including pushing Andie into Blaine's arms because he just might not be like other guys. (Although, see my first point for my real thoughts on that.)

So why is being Duckie such a bad thing?

Well, because he doesn't end up with Andie in the end.

# How to be a girl

I figured out very early in my boy-crazy life that the more of a tomboy I could be, the more I could actually talk to boys. So even though I may have occasionally curled my hair, worn makeup, made sure my belt always matched my shoes, wore skirts shorter than my dad would have liked, and rarely wore jeans, my topics of conversation always focused on boyish things: sports, comic books, video games, *Star Wars*. John Hughes once again provided an example that this would assure me lasting love, for if Watts (she actually wore men's underwear, for Pete's sake!) could finally land her Keith, then surely I (who wore pretty, silky women's underwear) could finally land my Keith.

My roommates at BYU my sophomore year were actually quite concerned about my tomboyish ways, and on a snowy Saturday in December, right before finals week, they took me to a mall in Salt Lake City. They decreed it "Turn Julie Into A Girl Day." I hadn't been on any dates that semester. Part of it was that I was still lamenting the loss of the boys I had met my freshman year, who were now all on church missions. Another part of it was that I had chosen to room with two of the most gorgeous girls I knew.

I've never quite understood how Nikki and Aimee

became my closest BYU friends, since I spent our entire BYU experience in their dating shadow. But I could always make them laugh, and if popular culture has taught us anything, it's that the pretty girls need a funny fat friend to help them get the guy. But Nikki and Aimee were the kind of girls who wanted me to have a guy, too. They didn't want me to sit in our dorm waiting for them to get home from dates. Hence the attempts to turn me into a real girl.

I figured their help was imperative; I'd already married off two roommates from my freshman year, with another one who was about to be engaged. To be honest, I was a bit panicked by the lack of dates. If I was going to be rescued from a lifetime of pariah-hood, I needed to embrace the finer things of femininity.

First stop: Victoria's Secret. I was 19 and had never been in a Victoria's Secret store. Before you judge me, remember that I lived in Nebraska and Montana for most of my teen years in the mid to late-1980s. We didn't have that store at any of the local malls. Them there stores were only in the big city. The giant photos of half-naked, skinny-yet-buxom women on the walls made me zip up my coat to my neck. I was a manatee among mermaids, a dandelion among roses, the most fantastical ugly duckling who had no swan DNA at all. My roommates held up lacy panty after lacy panty, frilly bra after frilly bra, and begged me to buy something.

"It will make you feel so much prettier!" they promised.

I wasn't sure how that would happen, as no one would see a lacy panty or frilly bra actually on me. And they were so expensive! Why would I spend my money on that? With Victoria's Secret a bust, we moved on to Crabtree and Evelyn, a bath and body store for the most discriminating of tastes. I'm positive my roommates intended this stop to be a little more low-key--that we would just try on different lotions and maybe pick up some bath salts, but all I remember is that everything there smelled like old lady. I used Caress or Tone soap that smelled like cocoa butter, reminding me of my few beach visits to California. Why did I need to spend $10 on a shower gel that wouldn't last nearly as long and reminded me of a nursing home? With the first two stops relative failures, we moved along to Nordstrom. My mission? Try on dresses.

It was horrible. Here's why: my roommates were both 5'8", slender, and perfectly proportioned. I was 5'3", not slender, and thanks to a mashup of Danish and Eastern European genes, I am not perfectly proportioned. They tried on gorgeous gowns and begged me to try on the same, but nothing fit right. If it fit in the chest, it draped past my toes. If it fit in the arms, it sagged across the midsection. After 20 minutes of playing dress up, I gave up, and told them I needed some air.

I meandered through Nordstrom, looking at various departments and watching families stroll in the aisles, when, like a foghorn leading a ship to shore in the dead of night, I heard it. It was faint at first. I stopped, bending my ear to determine which direction the sound was coming from. It was a crowd cheering. And though faint, I could also hear legendary sports announcer Keith

Jackson providing commentary. I followed the sound, and there in the corner of the men's department was a television showing a college football game.

Like a lighthouse showing a struggling sailor a clear path to a harbor, the sight and sound of the game guided me "home." Suddenly I was relaxed. I was happy. I was at peace, and I forgot all about frilly bras and lacy panties and elegant ball gowns. I stood there with a couple of abandoned husbands and boyfriends, and we watched the game. My roommates found me about 20 minutes later. They looked disappointed. For all of their efforts to turn me into a girl, I still ended up watching a football game with a bunch of guys.

I spent a lot of time at BYU hanging out with guys—going to football and basketball games, watching *SportsCenter* in the common room of the boys' dorm, and of course, setting them up with my much more feminine roommates. Though logic had no place in this social strata, I truly believed that if I spent time playing matchmaker, they would reciprocate. Surely they could think of at least one boy on a campus of 25,000 students that I'd be a good match with.

I had a class with my roommate Ruth's brother. His name was Lou, and he was so dreamy. Tan skin, light brown hair, the most chiseled jaw I'd ever seen, and visible muscles through his clothes. He was a god among mortals. Lou and I sat next to each other in Poli Sci 201, and would walk from the J. Reuben Clark Law Building to the main part of campus after class. We talked a lot during these walks, and when he visited his sister at our apartment, he and I would talk about everything from sports to politics.

After one particularly lively conversation, in which I made him laugh many times (all of us crushed on Lou so it was important to keep track of who he appeared to like the most), he said, "You are so cool. You're not like other girls. You're a pseudo-dude."

I'm sure Lou meant that as a compliment, but if there was ever a Watts-Keith moment in my life, that was it. I initially thought if my wit and intelligence might have made me appealing to Lou, then surely a lesser man could like me. His comment provided a glimmer of hope, that though I was pushing 20 years old, someone would whisk me away for a lifetime of wedded bliss. But even with that glimmer, a small part of my brain feared I'd be eternally sentenced to life as the friend, the tomboy that guys could talk to about anything, but never date.

Becoming best friends with boys actually wasn't difficult at all—in fact, it was quite easy. But I needed to find a balance somehow. Here are some simple steps to befriending a boy while simultaneously making him fall for you, as taught to me by Watts.

**1. Be mildly interested in the boy's interests.** Watts didn't have to draw like Keith did, but she was a musician. They shared a love of the arts. Having tangential but not identical interests let Watts be herself and didn't make her seem all stalkerish.

**2. Help him get the girl he thinks he wants.** Isn't it brilliant how Watts is so excited for Keith's date with Amanda Jones—so excited that she offers to chauffeur them? This combination of self-sacrifice and feigned disinterest I'm sure fascinated and confused Keith.

**3. Offer to give him kissing lessons.** Prior to his date with Amanda Jones, Watts asks Keith if he's confident in his kissing skills. Unconvinced of his answer, Watts guides Keith through a kiss that clearly rocked both their worlds. That moment was what Keith flashed to later in the film when he realized he really loved Watts, not Amanda.

I tried pulling a Watts once. Mr. Knightley and I had been on a couple of dates, and he was getting pretty gutsy with his level of flirting: walking up behind me and tickling my side, speaking to me with Natalie Imbruglia song lyrics, coupled with a general running subtext of how much he loved to make out. However, he made it clear we were only friends.

I happened to be driving us home from Dairy Queen one night, and about a block before his house was in sight, I pulled over, slammed the car in park, took off my seat belt, put my hands on his cheeks and kissed him. Terrified that he would push me away, I kept my eyes closed tight, hoping that my lips possessed enough spark to convince him I was worth kissing back. As soon as I felt his hands in my hair and down my neck, I dropped my hands from his cheeks and rested them on his chest, and he kissed me right back. After a good five minutes of kissing, I pulled away. He grinned.

"That was unexpected," he said.

I couldn't think of anything to say, so, blushing, I turned the key to start the car, and he put his hand on my hand.

"And it was nice. Thank you," he said.

By the end of that relationship he did not give me diamond earrings, so it appears Watts is a sucky teacher.

Bingley and I on a choir trip. He said I could use this photo. I think I wish he had not.

# Bingley

Bingley and I met in in Algebra III, which was the class for the cowards who didn't want to take pre-calc. He sat in front of me, and at first sight I was smitten. My 16-year-old self thought he was the most perfect creature to cross my path. I spent the better part of Algebra III ignoring Mr. Strom—who was a fine math teacher—and instead studied Bingley's hair, wondering what it would feel like between my fingers. Bingley was half Puerto Rican, and his dark wavy hair screamed out to me every day: "Touch me! Feel me!" When Mr. Strom blathered on about sine, cosine, and tangent, I leaned forward just enough to get a whiff of the musky cologne Bingley marinated in, hoping some of the scent would somehow transfer to my clothes so I could have that smell with me all the time. I imagined our first date—dinner at Wendy's and *License to Kill* at the movies—and tried to figure out how I could get him to ask me on that date. So I set out on a month-long quest to make him mine.

Step 1: Figure out what his interests were and take them as my own.

Luckily, this wasn't difficult because he liked sports, hip-hop, and singing, and I also liked those things.

"Who's your favorite football team?" I asked one day

as we walked from Algebra III to show choir.

"The Packers," he replied.

"The Packers? Too bad they don't have a decent quarterback."

"Oh yeah? Well who do you follow?" he countered.

"San Francisco, obviously. Best quarterback of all time," I said.

He rolled his eyes. "Bandwagon," he said, as he playfully punched my shoulder.

"Shut up," I punched back, as I reminded myself to not wash the shirt he had just touched.

One night as we drove around our tiny town looking for nothing to do, he popped in his Young MC cassette tape.

"You're gonna love this," he said, and he started rapping along to "Bust A Move."

"I love this song!" I shouted over the tinny but loud speakers.

"Let's learn all the words perfectly tonight," he suggested.

By the end of the night, I not only knew the words to "Bust A Move," but I also knew what the double entendres in the lyrics meant. Bingley was sweet enough to educate me on those, lest I look naive at the next school dance.

He was one of the first people to call me Jules on a regular basis, and once he christened me thus, I blanched when others who didn't know me as well used the same nickname. I mentioned once that if music didn't work out as a profession, I think I'd like to be a writer, so he began calling me Jules Verne. To this day, he's the only person who calls me that.

We were both in the select choir and the show choir. In the select choir, we sat in just the right spots so we could make faces at each other during rehearsals, though we refrained as much as possible out of respect for our director. The show choir graced me with opportunities to be his dance partner and actually touch him, be near him, and imagine he was singing to me.

It was almost too easy to worm my way into his life.

Step 2: Seek his help with math homework.

Math was the only class we had together that had actual homework, so it only made sense that I found ways to work on our math homework together. Unfortunately, I was slightly better at math than he was, so at times I would pretend to not know how to do my math homework so he could feel all masculine and Dudley Do-Right-ish. Of course, such help could only happen in the inner sanctum of his bedroom, so even if he could have helped me with the math, I wouldn't have retained a bit. Besides, most of the time he ended up playing Tecmo-Bowl on his Nintendo while I laid on my stomach on his bed, watching him defeat whatever NFL team was on the schedule for that day.

Step 3: Throw myself at him, with absolutely zero shame.

Despite being somewhat introverted, I'm actually pretty good at this. I can stalk with the best of them. I knew his schedule and made myself appear--always casually of course--in the same general area where he would walk at school. And since I was already at his side, we could walk to our classes together. I drove by his house, looking for his beige Ford Tempo parked by the curb, which I could take as an open invitation to "stop by." He never turned me away when I dropped in, uninvited. With all my spontaneous visits, I got to know his mom and dad—who both adored me and to this day I call "mom" and "dad"—and once I was in with his parents, I figured our coupledom was a given.

I followed these steps, and though my attraction to him never waned, all that time spent with him created a bond much deeper than a typical high school romance allowed. Bingley has a way of bringing people in and making them feel like they are the most important people in the room. I am pretty sure he knew I was smitten with him, much like Andie knew how Duckie felt about her. And rather than shatter my heart, Bingley found a way to forge a friendship with me that still is one of the most treasured relationships in my life. His mom once told me that she felt he had an old soul, that his capacity for loyalty and compassion wasn't found in most boys his age. These were qualities I longed for in a boyfriend, so even though I was disappointed when I realized he didn't like me "that way," I decided I would be his friend if he would have me. We were close—almost closer to each other than we were to our own significant others, so we managed to confuse people.

Early in our senior year of high school, an acquaintance from my drama class rushed to the stage and said, "Julie! I am so sorry! I don't want to be the one to tell you, but I just saw Bingley with another girl, and I'm pretty sure they're dating. So I yelled at him for you, because I cannot believe anyone would cheat on you."

It took me a second to process what she was saying because I knew Bingley had a girlfriend and I knew I was not she. I frowned, cocked my head to one side, and furrowed my brow.

Then she said, "You are dating him, right?"

I shook my head slowly and said, "No . . ."

Then she was the one with the confused expression on her face. She had seen Bingley and me in various casual situations and assumed we were dating because of how well we got along. Although, considering the typical angst present in teen relationships, our "getting along" probably should have hinted that we weren't dating. Bingley and I sobbed on graduation day; we called each other while at college—me at BYU, him at Concordia. Through college and as we started careers, we relied on each other through our failed relationships, even though we never lived in the same state. Before we both graduated from college, I visited him for a week. He didn't have a girlfriend at the time, and I was feeling hopeless about my own prospective romantic future. During that visit, we decided we would be each other's fall-back plan: if we were both single at 30, we would move in together and see what happened.

Two months before my 30th birthday, at intermission

of a high school concert I was playing in, I checked my voice mail. A message from Bingley:

"Dearest Jules Verne. Call me."

That was it.

I had 15 minutes to kill, so I summoned his number and waited.

"Hi there!"

"Hey, Julie!"

"So, what's up?"

"Not much. What are you doing?"

"Ah, just intermission at a concert. How about you?"

"I have a dilemma."

Ooh. Intrigue. Bingley is the most laid-back person I know, and rarely refers to anything as a dilemma. Plus, I felt a rush of giddiness at the prospect of being needed. No one had needed me in a long time, so I prepared to be brilliant.

"Okay, well, shoot," I began.

"See, I'm buying Ally an engagement ring—"

Let's stop right there, mainly because my brain at that moment forgot how to process information in a sane, rational, adult-like fashion. He blathered on about cut and clarity and the size of two diamonds, and he was torn over which he should buy. What would I want? He wanted to know.

"Well, I really don't think I'd care, so long as it resembled what I had in mind."

"Oh."

It wasn't what he was looking for, I could tell. But in retrospect, I don't think he really wanted me to help him decide which diamond he should buy; I think this was his gentle way of preparing me for what was coming.

"I'm asking Ally to marry me," he said.

I felt the sharp jolt of regret.

I blinked back tears, cleared my throat, and choked out, "I'm so happy for you."

And I was. But mixed in with that joy was a serving of loss, too. The house I'd imagined, the kids I'd named when I was eleven, the weekends spent cuddling on the couch—all of it evaporated as I listened to Bingley share his excitement of planning to ask this girl--this random girl I'd never even met—to spend the rest of her life with him.

Years later, during one of our catch-up phone calls, Bingley waxed nostalgic about how we have now been friends longer than we haven't been friends. He loves that about us. I'm not sure how he still holds me in such high regard—any attempt on my part to be at all self-deprecating with him is met with considerable evidence to the contrary. When I told him about the end to a relationship that I was still mourning, and wondering if I should try to contact said loser, he said I shouldn't. When I reassured him that I was much too cowardly to actually follow through, he chastised me.

"You? You are anything but cowardly. Look at how many things you've done in your life that required courage!"

I was Duckie—dependable, always available, ready to comfort him when a girl broke his heart—but I wanted to find a way to be Andie. The girl who was wanted by both Duckie and upper-class Blaine. The girl who didn't care what people thought. John Hughes never suggested that I'd be anything but hipster chic (before hipsters were hipster) yet completely desirable by all men, even the sleazy ones (I still can't look at James Spader and think anything but complete dirtbag). John Hughes did not prepare me for a lifetime of being Duckie. The friend. The confidant. And even though I completely identified with Andie's insecurities about her social class and knew in my heart I should have been her, throughout my entire life, I've been Duckie to several men I really, really liked.

At the end of *Pretty in Pink*, Duckie hooks up with the girl who would later play the movie version of *Buffy the Vampire Slayer*. So for all we know, Duckie ended his prom night with a wooden stake to his heart.

# Wickham

Once Bingley and I settled into the most platonic of all platonic love, I had to find my next possibility. John Hughes taught me that being alone was weak; serial monogamy justified my womanhood. Though only 16 years old, the message I got from church was that I had a mere three years to finally get married. Timing was crucial and did not allow me the luxury of pining for Bingley, not when my eggs were at risk of drying up. With John Hughes on one shoulder and my church on the other, I set my sights on Wickham, Bingley's best friend. Wickham was Bingley's polar opposite. Moody, sullen, defiant to authority. Listened to The Cure, Depeche Mode, and The Smiths. An avid runner and rabid sports fan, Wickham was emo dressed in jock clothing. He fascinated me. Despite his lanky frame and pockmarked face, I thought he was hot. Hotter than Bingley, even. I admired him from afar for a month, noting his moods, listening to his lunchtime conversations to try and find my in. After a month, I was still too afraid to approach until fate intervened one gorgeous November day at a choir festival.

The festival was comprised of most of the select high school choirs in the state, directed by a professor from a college. During one of our breaks, the professor instructed, "Find someone you've never spoken to before, and learn something about that person."

I know the professor's intent was for me to talk to someone from Billings, Missoula, or even Kalispell, but on my way to that side of the gym, Wickham appeared in my path.

"I've never really talked to you," he said.

I may have peed myself a little. The boy I had spent weeks idolizing, fantasizing about, and sure, stalking a bit, was actually speaking to me.

"Well then, I guess this counts," I said.

I wish I could remember the remainder of our conversation, but all I remember is the end:

"Here's my phone number. You should call me tonight," he said, pressing a piece of scratch paper into my hand.

I opened it. He had horrible handwriting.

"Is that a '2'?" I asked.

"Yeah."

"Oh. Okay. Yeah, I'll call you," I said, and floated back to the alto section.

That night, I called him, and in traditional teen fashion, we talked for over an hour about everything and nothing. I was hooked. He was funny, dry, sarcastic, and much smarter than his grades suggested. We talked most nights on the phone, started to hang out in show choir, and he seemed to go out of his way to see me between classes at school. We were on the path to true teen love.

Our school had two proms a year—senior prom in

December, junior in April. He didn't want to go to senior prom, so instead I went to his house and we watched *I'm Gonna Git You Sucka*. Not the most romantic film, and truthfully, it was not a film my parents would have approved of at all. But I was AT HIS HOUSE. On his couch. So close to him I could hear him breathe and laugh and it was all I could do to keep my hands and face off of him. When I left that night, he told me he was spending the holiday break in California, where his mom lived.

"I'll call you when I get back in town," he promised.

He gave me a hug, then opened his front door so I could leave. Halfway to my car, I turned around and saw his lanky figure leaning against the doorframe, a half-grin on his face as he watched me walk to my car. On the 20-minute drive home, I wondered how I was going to survive the next two weeks. Long-distance calls were expensive, and it's not like we were serious or exclusive or that I deserved a phone call from California. Though in my mind I couldn't see how he would want to call anyone else.

Two days before he was supposed to come home, as I lay love-stricken on the couch watching *Days of Our Lives,* the phone rang.

"Hello?"

"Hi. Is Julie there?"

"This is she," I said. It sounded like Wickham, but it was the middle of the afternoon on a Monday, when long-distance charges were most expensive. Surely he wouldn't call me in the middle of the afternoon on a Monday.

"Hey, it's Wickham."

A boy I liked was calling me from California at 3:45 p.m. This was serious stuff now.

We chatted for 30 minutes about what we got for Christmas and how we'd been spending time on our break, and then he said, "I can't wait to get back to Montana."

"I can't wait to see you," I said.

"See you in a couple of days," he said.

"Okay. Bye."

Upon his return, we had a magical two weeks. Two solid weeks of three-hour phone conversations, two weekends driving around Great Falls in his silver Jeep Cherokee, never touching each other, but constantly flirting and casting Jane Austen-worthy longing glances. After an evening of tickle fights and cuddling and still not knowing what I meant to him, I asked what we were doing.

"Well, how do you feel?" he asked.

"I like you. A lot. You're the only guy I feel so strongly about right now, and I think we could be a really good couple."

Being that straightforward was new to me, and my stomach flipped and my lungs stopped giving me breath while I waited for his response.

"Well, I just want to be friends," he said.

"Oh. Yeah. I mean, that's . . . yeah . . . okay. So I should get back home before my parents get angry with me."

"Are you okay? Tell me you're okay."

"I'mfinenoworriesbutIreallyhavetogosobye."

He stood in his doorway and watched me leave, so I couldn't start crying until I was halfway down his block. Much like Duckie tries to cut Andie out of his life when she starts seeing Blaine, I cut Wickham out of mine. For two weeks we did not talk in choir or on the phone. For two weeks I convinced myself I did not like him. For two weeks, even though he bought me lunch (an orange juice and a fruit roll-up), I was impervious. Ice Queen. And I needed to be, because at the end of January the show choir was heading to Missoula for a festival, and I did not want to risk a weekend with him so near to me resulting in a complete reversal of my commitment to forget him.

The day we left for Missoula, I boarded the charter bus and staked out a seat. The bus had double the seats we actually needed, so I put a pillow and blanket in the seat next to me. Wickham boarded the bus, saw me, and asked if he could sit next to me.

"No," I replied, and buried my eyes in a book.

"Please?"

"Why?" I asked, without looking up.

"I want to talk to you," he said.

I looked up and shot him my best "go away" face. His puppy-dog brown eyes pleaded, but he knew better than to smile. He actually looked pained, genuine. I held his gaze for a few seconds, cocked my eyebrow and rolled my eyes as he eventually broke into a grin. He knew I would say yes. He knew he was my Achilles Heel.

"Fine," I sighed, and moved my pillow and blanket.

He settled in next to me, and rambled about

basketball and music and his step-mom and school, and before long, he had snuggled close to me and was softly snoring. I was too confused to sleep.

Maybe he misses me, I thought. Maybe he wants to go back to two weeks ago, I hoped.

But the rational side of my brain prevailed, and I pushed away any possibility of reconciliation. Bingley and a few other guys behind me peeked over my seat, saw Wickham sleeping and asked if I wanted to hang out with them at the mall where we were stopping for dinner. I nodded, and as I watched the Montana prairie morph into Montana mountains during the three-hour bus ride, sitting so close to him I knew my shirt would smell like Brut 66 cologne for days, the rational gave way to fantasy, and I imagined my immediate future with Wickham.

Scene One: He wakes up. I tell him, "You're the one who just wanted to be friends. Don't for a second treat me like a tawdry Choir Trip Romance to keep you occupied this weekend. Leave me alone for the rest of the trip."

Scene Two: He wakes up. He tells me, "I was wrong to only give us such a short period of time. No other girl compares to you. I was foolish to tell you we should just be friends. I love you. Always." And he would exit the bus, leaving me to decide if his speech would be worthy of a second chance. Irritated by its triteness, I would decide it was not worthy.

I prepared for Scene One, and waited for him to wake up.

When we arrived at the mall, Wickham woke up and

asked, "Where do you want to go for dinner?"

"Oh. I'm going with Bingley, Josh, Justin, and Wayne," I said.

"Can we go somewhere for dinner? Just the two of us? I want to spend time with you."

Those words rattled around in my brain. I wanted to believe he was sincere. I don't know why I had such a blind spot for him—he wasn't an Adonis, wasn't at all ambitious. In fact, he was tortured, mysterious, aloof, a little pathetic, not immediately attractive.

Though I was only a junior in high school, I could sense my 25-year-old self reaching through time to tell me, "No. He will hurt you. You are better than this."

Wickham and the group I'd agreed to go to dinner with shivered as they waited for me to make up my mind. January in Missoula isn't tropical, and I needed to make a choice. In the cliché battle between heart and mind, heart won easily, and Wickham and I spent the evening at the Missoula Mall. The next day we were inseparable during breaks and meals. It was dark by the time we left Missoula, and as we once again sat together on the bus, he put his arm around me and pulled me close. We looked at the stars, and he pointed out Orion.

"Now, every time you look at Orion, you'll think of me," he said.

I sighed and relaxed into his chest.

"You're my best friend, Julie. I really love you. I don't want you to not be part of my life."

I smiled so big my cheeks hurt, and for a split-second, I worried he could see my reaction. I didn't want him to know how happy he made me. I wanted to match his typical aloofness with equal aloofness. With nothing but a three-hour drive in the dark ahead of us, we dozed and snuggled. When we got back to the school, he walked me to my car.

"I'll see you tomorrow. We can watch the Super Bowl together," he said.

"Okay. See you then," I said.

He hugged me tight—but did not kiss me—and I drove home with an immovable grin.

This time I was not going to be Duckie after all.

Eighteen hours later, Wickham was in my basement, watching the San Francisco 49ers play in the Super Bowl. He was on one end of the couch; I was on the other end. He wouldn't look at me. I tried to move closer to him, and he would get a drink or go to the bathroom. His avoidance was clear, though I didn't want to believe it. Nor would it be the last time in my life he would use similar tactics.

At halftime, I asked him what was going on.

"Well, I'm seeing Becky from Great Falls High," he said.

My stomach lurched and I could feel tears brimming, and even though I was a weak 16-year-old who let a boy play me for two days, I did not want him to see me cry. So instead, I narrowed my eyes, uncrossed my legs, leaned forward and said, "I guess I should take you home, then."

I flounced up the basement stairs, slamming doors in my wake. I waited in the car to take him home. He opened the passenger-side door, climbed in, and we drove the 20 minutes to his house in complete silence. But in my head, I was screaming at him.

Why spend all weekend with me? Why were you so insistent on being back in my life again? Why hold me and show me that dumb constellation? And for the love of all that is holy, why tell me you love me? What was this weekend all about? I was fine until I let you sit next to me. Is it control? Is it power? Are you just deranged? And isn't Becky a freshman (she was) and isn't that gross? What is so wrong with me that you've decided twice in the past four weeks that I'm not good enough for you?

But my 16-year-old self lacked the assertiveness to demand an explanation for the weekend. My 16-year-old self didn't think to fight for someone she loved. I didn't know what that looked like—when Duckie realizes Andie doesn't love him "that way", he doesn't fight for Andie, he fights with her. When Andie realizes Blaine has blown her off for prom, she doesn't fight for him, she fights with him. And I didn't want to start a fight with Wickham, and I didn't want to tell him he was making a mistake by letting me go, so when we arrived at his house, he simply got out of the car, shut the door, and walked to his front door.

Turn around, I willed. Turn around, look at me, and see what you're throwing away.

But he never slowed as he approached the door. He just turned the doorknob, walked inside, and shut the door. Just like that, we were over . . . again. I sat in the driveway for a few seconds in case he changed his mind, flung open the door and ran to my car. But the seconds were dangerously approaching a minute, and that's when the first tear rolled down my cheek, soon followed by choking sobs. I drove the quarter-mile to Bingley's house, into Bingley's comforting arms. He let me listen to "Look Away" and "Will You Still Love Me" and "Hard Habit to Break" repeatedly, and I cried for four hours.

It was the first time I grappled with crushed self-esteem. Wickham wasn't all that cute or ambitious and even he didn't want me. At 16, I felt the first possibility that I would always be alone. It was a fleeting thought—after all, every week at church I was told I'd be married. Only completely ugly losers couldn't get married, and I didn't see myself as completely ugly. The initial terror of thinking I would be single forever was quickly dismissed by "God wouldn't do that to me" followed by "Even Duckie ends up with someone at prom."

I wish I could say this was the only time Wickham broke my heart. I wish I could say that I was as strong as Amanda Jones at the end of *Some Kind Of Wonderful*, when she asserts her independence. But instead, I became like Lloyd Dobler. Wickham was my Diane Court, and every time he walked into the boxing gym of my life, I ended up flat on my back with a broken nose.

Metaphorically speaking, of course.

Two weeks later, on Valentine's Day, sometime between English and show choir, I went to my locker. An envelope fell to the ground. Wickham's now-familiar chicken scratch handwriting was on the front. I looked around to see if he was lurking behind another set of lockers, but he was nowhere to be found. I opened the envelope, and inside was a card. On the front, a photo of a man with horn-rimmed glasses and slicked-back black hair. He sported a black and white houndstooth jacket, an off-white shirt, and a red bow tie. The man wore a huge smile and clenched a rose in his teeth.

I opened the card. It read: "The stud-lord of passion has consented to being your Valentine again this year. (Oooh . . . you are one lucky person.)"

Below that was this: "Julie--I thought this card is really fitting and when I looked at it, I thought of you. Happy Valentine's Day. Wickham (p.s. you ARE one lucky person . . . again)"

Why he gave me a Valentine's Day card two weeks after he broke my heart is still a mystery. But it established the practice of former boyfriends contacting me and asking me to be in their lives long after they broke my heart.

That all happened in 1990, and it wasn't until 2001 that I was able to shake Wickham for good. In 1992 we dated again, talked about marriage, decided the timing wasn't right, and two weeks later he was dating my sister Deanne. I initially hesitated to write about it, as I have spent many a Thanksgiving rehashing these events with Deanne in true family-drama form. But Deanne read an early draft of this book and said, "You should give more details about that summer."

"Really?" I asked.

"Oh yeah! It totally plays into how you really were Duckie to Wickham's Andie," she said.

"Hm. Yeah, I guess I could add that," I said.

"Besides, it's the only way I'm going to be in your book," she said.

So, ladies and gentlemen, I give you . . .

"The Summer of our Discontent"

Me and my sister Deanne, in Bingley's basement.

Despite the initial heartbreak during our junior year of high school, Wickham and I ended high school as friends. Good friends, even. Senior year, Wickham, Bingley, and I would occasionally ditch our significant others and have an evening just us. Just friends. While I was at BYU, Wickham was at school in California and we often wrote letters and exchanged mixtapes. Coming back to Great Falls after our freshman years of college, we were both single. One of our high school friends got married that summer, so Wickham and I went to the reception together. After that reception, he and I started hanging out almost every day. It was completely casual—movies, dinners, Tecmo-Bowl marathons, baseball games, *SportsCenter*—and I enjoyed the easiness of being with him. We weren't at all physical in our affection for each other, but several nights he drove us around town in that same silver Jeep Cherokee as we talked about our clichéd hopes and dreams. I wouldn't necessarily call what we did "dating," but we weren't spending time with anyone else, either. After two months of seeing each other every day, we went to a church dance together. I didn't think of it as a date. It was just another Friday night with Wickham.

Mormon dances are quite the cultural phenomenon. First of all, they take place in the church gym. Activity committees do their best to spruce up the place with streamers, balloons, and low lighting. But the minute you look at your feet, you might see a free throw line or a three-point arc, and the magic wears off a bit.

Mormon dances for singles in Montana were a bit of

a joke after going to dances at BYU. I was used to a crowd of at least a thousand, so when Wickham and I arrived to a group of about 30, I knew any fun I was about to have would be of my own making. We sat out the "Boot Scootin' Boogie" (sidenote: I forgot that in Montana there would likely be no Nine Inch Nails played at the dance, like at BYU), and I sipped nervously at warm punch as we talked about politics and movies. For all the lack of aesthetics, I grew up believing Mormon dances held magic powers. Nothing inherently Mormon convinced me of this, instead, again, my friends John Hughes and Jane Austen managed that for me.

It's at prom where Andie and Blaine finally reconnect and fall in love. It's at a ball where Elizabeth Bennet and Mr. Darcy initially spar, the catalyst for their affection. And since Mormon dances happened frequently throughout high school and college, surely the Law of Averages would catch up to me and provide an equally magical moment. So even though Wickham and I had settled into a companionship of comfort that summer, my nerves had me on high alert that night. Finally, a slow song came on, and he asked me to dance.

He put my right hand on his chest and covered it gently with his left hand, while his right arm wrapped around my waist and rested on the small of my back. My left hand reached up to rest on his shoulder, and we shuffled our feet back and forth while Richard Marx serenaded us with "Right Here Waiting" over the sound system. An apt song as, by this point, I had been in love with Wickham for three years. I initially concentrated over Wickham's shoulder, scanning the room for the Unfortunates who were not asked to dance during this song. Girls with stringy hair who hadn't mastered the art of using makeup and boys in pants with hems just a smidgen too high, none of them daring to talk to each other, lined the back wall and stared at the couples on the dance floor, as if we had all figured out some grand secret to swaying back and forth with someone we liked. Focusing on them grounded me, reminded me that in truth, that was where I belonged. Not dancing with Wickham, certainly not to this song. But my devils eventually silenced my better angels, and I shifted my gaze to Wickham. He smiled at me, and my knees buckled.

I felt a gravitational pull to rest my head on his shoulder, yet somehow I defied that law of relationship physics and focused on an escaped streamer floating down from the basketball hoop. An instinct told me to slowly move a little closer to him, but instead I took a step back. My left hand, with a mind of its own, started to reach for the nape of his neck to play with the brown curls that needed to be cut. But the Missoula trip from a year and a half earlier flashed in my memory, and I moved my hand to rest on his bicep instead, to create distance.

Just friends, I told myself. We are just friends.

I don't remember what he said to make me cackle with laughter, but I remember he added: "I'm just trying to be witty to impress you."

"You don't need to impress me," I said.

The song ended, and rather than immediately separate, we stood on the dance floor a moment longer. I wanted to suggest that we leave, but I didn't have an idea of where we could go to continue what I thought had started during that dance.

"Wanna get out of here?" he asked.

"Yes," I said.

We headed to Bingley's house to play pool. Bingley was at work and his parents were out of town, so we had the house to ourselves. We played in relative awkward silence, and my mind raced with why we weren't talking. Maybe during that slow dance, he could tell what I was thinking and now he was looking for a way out. Or maybe he could tell what I was thinking and he was thinking the same things. Either option terrified me. After he sank the eight ball, he put his cue on the table and sat on the basement stairs. I walked over to him.

"What's wrong?" I asked.

"Why?" he asked.

"Why what?" I said.

"Why we?" he asked.

"Is there a 'we'?" I countered.

"I don't know. Sometimes, I guess," he said, and he dropped his head into his hands.

I stepped toward him, obeying all those laws of physics I defied at the dance. I put my hands on his shoulders, then slowly moved my hands around his neck and stroked his hair. He pulled me closer and rested his hands on my hips, his head pressing gently into my stomach. We stayed that way, silent, for several minutes.

I couldn't say anything to him. We had been here before, and I knew how much it could hurt. I was going to let him direct this version of our play. He finally looked up at me.

"It's too late, isn't it? I'm already in love," he said.

He stood up, wrapped his arms around me and kept me close. It was getting late, so he grabbed my hand, walked me upstairs, and drove me home. We held hands for the entire drive. He walked me to my front door.

"Are you tired? Can I come in?" he asked.

"No, I'm not tired. Come in," I said.

We sat on the couch, still holding hands, and talked for two hours. In the wee hours of the morning, I walked him to the door hoping he would finally kiss me after three years, but he didn't. He gave me another sweet and gentle hug, touched my face, and left.

He is the one boy I loved who never kissed me.

After that night, we still saw each other, but the ease of just being together was no longer there. A week later, my family went on our annual camping trip to Glacier National Park, so we didn't see each other for three days—the longest we'd gone without seeing each other all summer.

When we returned from Glacier, he told me we shouldn't get serious. He was planning to serve a mission for our church, and he didn't want to be tempted to not go because of me. This was sound reasoning—I wanted him to serve a mission. He also wasn't the first boy I'd sacrificed for my faith. It's an expectation. Much like the image of a 1940s canteen girl valiantly sending her sweetheart off to war, I'd already dutifully waved goodbye to two potential suitors as they left for two years of missionary service. Wickham would simply be the third, and admittedly, the most difficult to send off. So I was more than confused when, a week later, he started dating my sister Deanne.

I don't know how they got together in the first place. Deanne was around quite a bit that summer, so it may have been an organic development. Then again, she was two years younger than me, taller, thinner, tanner, blonder, more athletic, less dramatic, and way more carefree than I was. I expected to lose boyfriends to my roommates at BYU, who were also taller, thinner, tanner, and blonder than me. I never thought I'd lose one to my sister, though. At the beginning of August, after he had taken Deanne out on several dates, I couldn't take it anymore. I couldn't understand why, after the history we'd had to this point, he would be so purposefully hurtful to me. And though I preferred the path of least resistance when it came to my relationships, we had been too close, had been through too much for him to not tell me what he was thinking. So one night I demanded an explanation. Here is my journal entry from that evening:

*August 8, 1992*
*Went to his house last night and goofed off and then we got in a discussion about him and me and Deanne. He's "falling into the pit of love" but catches himself at the last minute—in relation to me. PIT OF LOVE? My heck. If he was any cornier I might have*

*to hurl. He turned around and in the same breath said he was head over heels for Deanne. Hello? What is going on?*

I went back to BYU three weeks later, desperately trying to convince myself I did not care if I talked to Wickham ever again, but hoping his fling with Deanne was indeed just a fling and that he'd want a return to a substantive relationship with me soon. And as he did every time we hit rough patches, he wormed his way back into my life. Letters and mixtapes flew between Utah and California, because just like Duckie can't leave Andie alone for prom, I was never very good at completely abandoning Wickham. The fling with my sister did not last, and he was actually a little heartbroken at its conclusion. He left for his mission in May 1993. We wrote often in the two years he was gone, and when he returned, I took a trip to Great Falls to spend time with him and Bingley. Just like old times: him, vacillating between flirtatious and aloof; me, heartwrenchingly lovelorn.

Andie and Duckie.

In 1997, in the dead of winter, he drove from Montana to Nebraska to see me before I left for my mission. My dad admitted to me later that he thought for sure Wickham was going to propose and I wouldn't go on my mission. While boys are expected to serve missions, girls are not, and I had heard more than one story of girls all set to walk into the Missionary Training Center, only to be stopped by boys who, finally facing 18 months without them, proposed. I was kind of hoping for that, too. Instead, we spent a weekend playing Trivial Pursuit (something we did every time we were together), ice skating, and watching movies. I asked him over and over if I would even survive my mission. After his tenth reassurance that I was going to be fine, he looked at me.

"What?" I asked.

"Nothing," he said.

"Then why are you looking at me?" I asked.

He paused, sighed, and reached for my hand.

"Can't I just look at you?"

I blushed, and in that moment didn't want to cry, so I broke into a big smile and threw my head back on the couch. Seconds later, I slid onto his shoulder, and we sat in silence, close, just like we had seven years earlier on a bus to Missoula.

The morning I left for my mission, Wickham wanted to get an early start on his drive back to Montana. We stood on the landing of my parents' split-level home. I couldn't help crying this time. Emotion made Wickham very uncomfortable, but he held me anyway.

"I've never seen you this upset," he whispered.

I sobbed harder.

I've often thought about why I was crying so much that morning. Part of it was the unknown—had I known how hard my mission in Quebec was going to be, I probably would not have gone. I knew I would miss my family terribly. I worried that I'd never finish college once I left. And I knew many of those tears were shed because I was telling Wickham goodbye for possibly the rest of my life. Eighteen months was a long time, and I was certain he would get married while I was gone. Saying goodbye to him that morning meant saying goodbye to the hope of a life with him. It hurt. He promised to write me as often as he could, and every letter I got from him was a treasure. Especially one that arrived six weeks before the end of my mission.

"Hey, wanna get married after you get home? If you said yes, call me the second you are released."

At the end of the letter, he wrote out one of Shakespeare's love sonnets, and said he'd see me soon. Less than two months later, Wickham made the Montana to Nebraska trek again to see me when I returned from my mission. He rolled into town around 10 p.m.
I threw open the front door.

"Wickham!" I screamed, and I threw my arms around him.

His arms hung lamely at his sides, and after a couple of seconds, I felt one of them pat me on the back while the other one pushed me away.

"Hey," he said.

I looked at him, puzzled. It had been 18 months, and he had essentially proposed the idea of marrying me not two months earlier. Shouldn't he be more excited to see me?

I thought he might be tired, so I showed him to the room where he would be sleeping. As we walked down the hall, he told me about a girl he had a crush on in Montana. I'd not seen him in 18 months, and I'd not been a missionary for six hours. I'd been anticipating seeing him especially since his quasi-proposal six weeks

51

earlier, and his first conversation starter was about a crush? Not wanting to push him away, I let him talk while offering the occasional "Mmmhmmm" and told myself that his crush didn't matter; he was with me right now, and we were going to have a magical two weeks together. Given those initial moments of his visit, I don't know why I was surprised by the events of the next three days. Conversation lagged. He told me he was never getting married. He said, "I feel like we have so much to talk about, but now that I'm here, I don't know what to say."

And after three days, I'd had enough and as we drove into the city, I asked him. Point blank.

"Are we going to talk about your proposal?"

He nearly choked on his soda. "What proposal?" he said.

"The one you sent me in a letter six weeks ago. When you said you'd been thinking and that we should get married."

"That?" he said. I'll never forget the look on his face; I was reading two different emotions. He was trying so hard to hide that he had meant it, that he had considered it, while simultaneously trying to convince me he couldn't, not in a million years, ever think of marrying me.

"That was a joke. I'm not at all attracted to you."

"What?"

"Well, I suppose on paper we're a pretty good match, and we have great conversations, but I'm just not attracted to you. I never have been," he said.

"Then what about all the letters you wrote to me the

last 18 months? Each one got increasingly affectionate," I said.

"You're reading too much into them. You always do that. It's your fatal flaw," he said.

"How should I read into 'Wanna get married when you get home?'" I yelled.

"Well, you can't take everything I say at face value," he said.

I have never in my life wanted an eject button for the passenger seat more than that moment.

"You're leaving tomorrow," I said.

"But what about going to the Field of Dreams? And Bingley is coming up too! I can't leave tomorrow," he argued.

"You can stay to see Bingley for one meal, and then I want you gone," I said.

Instead of going into the city, I drove us back to the house, where he went on a walk by himself and I retreated to my bedroom and cried.

He left the next day, and I avoided his phone calls for two months. Every time I avoided a phone call, a couple of days later a package would arrive from Amazon. A Calvin and Hobbes book. A coffee table book of Georgia O'Keeffe's paintings. A book of philosophy by Jacques Derrida. I liked the Calvin and Hobbes book. I hate paintings of flowers, and I detest French deconstructionists. But I kept the books anyway, because at the end of the day, they reminded me of Wickham, and I missed him terribly. It took a year until we were back to some semblance of normalcy, or whatever you call the status quo for Wickham and me, and we were friends again.

In 2000 he moved to Utah, not long after I did, and we would hang out occasionally. At first, it was awkward—talking to him long-distance was one thing, talking to him in person reminded me how much I loved him, and probably always would. So about once a month, we would go see a movie. I would be as charming as possible, laugh at his jokes, leave my hand closest to him completely free and open in case he wanted to hold it. Yet again, all I wanted was for him to want me, and he didn't.

Since Wickham and I lived in the same state, Bingley thought it would be a nice time to visit, and he arranged to be in Utah for my 28th birthday.

"Don't plan anything," Bingley told me. "We got this. It'll be a great day."

I woke up with flu-like symptoms on my birthday that year, but forced myself to get out of bed around 9 a.m. and get ready for the day. Bingley was staying with Wickham in a town about 90 minutes from me, and I had no clue what time they were coming or what they had planned. At 10:30, I thought they might call. At 11:30, I started to worry, so I called Wickham's house. No answer. By 12:30 I was pissed, so I called Wickham's house again (neither he nor Bingley had cell phones).

"Yeah," a sleepy Bro-mate voice said.

"Hi, is Wickham there?" I asked through gritted teeth.

"Nah, man, he's out golfing," replied the Bro-mate.

"Um, do you know what his tee-time was? Or what

time he'll be back?"

"Nah, man. I just woke up."

"Okay then. Will you write this down? Julie called. She said don't come to Salt Lake, something came up. Got that?"

"Yeah, got it," Bro-mate said.

I stewed for a few minutes, trying to figure out what I could do with my day. I had jettisoned all my other friends—friends who wanted to take me to lunch and to the movies—because Bingley and Wickham promised me a great day. My birthday is a Utah state holiday, so most of my friends didn't have to work that day. Once I cut them loose from birthday duty, they made other plans. But I was not going to sit at home all day and wallow. Instead, I went to Victoria's Secret and got a makeover with their new line of makeup.

When I returned from Victoria's Secret and other shopping stops, Bingley and Wickham were sitting on my porch. I said nothing to either of them but let them in, and I marched straight up to my room where I chatted online for 20 minutes with on old friend from high school. When I came back downstairs, Bingley sprung up to talk to me, while Wickham stayed sitting, staring into the carpet.

"I'm so so so so so sorry. I thought Wickham told you about the golfing," Bingley started.

"I don't want to hear it," I said. "I left a message for you to not come down here; did you not get it?"

"No, we got it," Bingley said, half-hanging his head.

"Then why are you here?" I asked.

"Because it's your birthday," Bingley said.

By this time, it was nearing 6 p.m., and I had spent my entire birthday alone. In the years since then, I've spent an occasional birthday alone by choice. But that year, I was so looking forward to Bingley's visit. I was disappointed that he let Wickham hijack my day and so tired of Wickham's emotional assaults over the years that I saw only one option.

"I think you should leave," I said.

Wickham finally piped up, "We drove an hour and a half to get here!"

I glared at him.

"Please, just let us take you to dinner," Bingley begged.

"No. You need to leave now. I'm way too angry to enjoy any time with you, and I might be able to at least piece together a dinner with some friends if I start making phone calls now," I said.

Wickham got up off the couch, walked out the door and into his car.

Bingley gave me a hug and cried a little as he apologized again for ruining my birthday.

"It's not your fault," I said. "It's Wickham. It's always Wickham."

Two months later on a Saturday morning as I drove to school so I could work on lesson plans, I waited for a light to change so I could turn left. I remember the light turning yellow. I remember seeing a truck about a quarter-mile away and thinking, "He won't run this light."

He ran the light.

Or so said the witnesses; I was unconscious for the better part of the day. The truck apparently gunned it when he saw the light turn, and his headlights ended up near the gearshift in my little Mercury Tracer. I was lucky that the only bone I broke was my nose. Shards of glass embedded in my scalp, and it took four staples to close the wounds. The concussion was no picnic, either.

Two weeks later, still jacked up on pain meds, Wickham showed up at my house. My sister had told Bingley about my accident and since he was living in North Carolina, he asked Wickham if he would drive to Salt Lake and check up on me. Perhaps Wickham thought that if I was hopped up on Percocet I'd be unable to still be angry with him. So on a random Saturday, he called and said he was in Salt Lake, said Bingley had told him about my accident, said he wanted to see me. The Percocet said, "Sure, come on over!"

I was not prepared for what I would see when he rang my doorbell.

He brought a girl with him.

I invited them in, took the flowers and card they brought, and Wickham excused himself to the restroom, leaving me with the flavor of the week.

"So," I said, "you live in Logan?"

"Yeah," she replied.

"Are you going to school?"

"No."

"Oh. So, where do you work?"

"I don't."

"Oh. You're just living in Logan?"

"Yep."

Even in my drugged state, I was floored that this Goddess of Apathy existed. I had always thought, and at times dreamed, about what people who did nothing looked like. She was young, thin, but rather plain in her appearance. Blond hair, but not too blond. Styled but functional. And she was so quiet. Even on Percocet, I could still hold a conversation. This girl showed no signs of being under the influence of narcotics, and she barely spoke. The rest of the visit is blurred by drugs and disappointment, and I didn't hear from Wickham again until one night two months later, when he called asking for my address.

"If you need my address to send me a wedding invitation, don't bother. I won't go."

"Why not?"

"I can't watch you marry someone else. I can't do it," I said.

"But you're the closest thing I have to family who can be there. No one in my family can be in the temple," he reasoned.

For a moment, I felt badly. Wickham joined the LDS church his freshman year of college, much to his family's dismay. He wasn't exaggerating that I really was the closest LDS family he had. But I couldn't imagine myself sitting in the Oakland Temple, watching him pledge his life to someone else for time and all eternity. I couldn't watch someone else get the life I wanted, the life I wanted with him.

The 16-year-old in me, the Duckie, wanted to say,

"Yes. I'll be the lovelorn martyr, put on a happy face and watch the life I want—the life I deserve—vanish." But I wasn't 16 anymore. I was 28. And it was time to act like it.

"I'm sorry," I said. "I just can't do it."

He didn't send me an invitation, and we didn't talk again until three years later, at Bingley's Wedding.

# Bingley's Wedding

Going to Wickham's wedding would have been emotionally destructive, but not going to Bingley's Wedding would have been just as emotionally destructive. So once I recovered from the initial shock of Bingley's engagement, I planned out how I would spend the year prior to his wedding.

1. Go tanning. He'd be getting married in July in North Carolina. I spent time in the South as a young teenager and remembered the importance of beautiful femininity. I must be tan.

2. Find the perfect outfit. Again, anticipating subtle judgments of the Southern women who would attend the wedding, I knew I needed the perfect dress, shoes, and purse. Everything needed to match; the dress needed to flatter and slim, while the shoes needed to add a little height. The purse needed to be big enough to carry essentials but small enough to tell people I was not a high maintenance kind of girl.

3. Lose 40 pounds. I had a better chance of finding the perfect outfit if I didn't have to shop at Ye Olde Tent Dress and MuuMuu Store for Women; I also had a better chance of not breaking down in front of Wickham—Bingley's best man—if I was confident in my appearance. As the wedding neared, I threw in blonde highlights and

a good supply of M.A.C. cosmetics to ensure Wickham would feel at least one pang of regret at not marrying me.

The only parts of the plan that worked were the tan and the outfit. Against all conventional medical wisdom, I spent the summer in a tanning bed, and was nicely bronzed by the time Bingley's Wedding rolled around. I found a black floral print knee-length wrap dress, paired it with black patent leather slingback sandals and a small black clutch to hold my ID, some cash, lip gloss, and my cell phone. Physically, despite not dropping the 40 pounds, I was ready for Bingley's Wedding. When I arrived at Bingley's house, I realized I had failed to make sure I was emotionally prepared for what the weekend would bring.

A couple of weeks before Bingley's Wedding, he asked me if I was going to be okay with Wickham there. Was I "past all that old stuff?"

I sighed and hesitated. "I think I am," I said.

"You think you are?" Bingley asked.

"Well, I'm not sure what he and I have been through is something I'll ever really be over. I loved him so fiercely, and for so long, only to be hurt over and over again . . . that's not something that just disappears, you know?"

Now it was Bingley's turn to sigh and pause. "I know. I just wish it was different. You two are my best friends."

"I know. He was my best friend too for a while. And I know it was my choice to cut him out of my life when I wouldn't go to his wedding. But I don't think you blame me for that, do you?" I asked.

"No, no, I don't. I know how hard that would've been for you," Bingley said.

"I'll admit, I'm surprised that three years have passed and I still have days that I mourn that relationship. But I can promise you this: I won't make a scene, and I will play nice, and if I am tempted to cry, I will tell anyone who asks that I'm just so happy for you and Ally. Sound good?" I said.

"Sounds good," Bingley said.

I knew it would be weird seeing Wickham after three years of silence, and decided I'd take cues from him as to how to react. Bingley wanted me to go from the airport straight to his house, so I fought through the rainy Fourth of July weekend traffic, and arrived at around 4:45 p.m. I knocked, and no one answered. So I rang the doorbell, and heard someone bounce down the stairs. A paper-thin girl with a short trendy bob and glasses answered the door. I tried to place her, especially since she was wearing a blue Salt Lake Community College t-shirt. Didn't expect many of those in North Carolina.

"Hi! I'm Julie."

"Oh. Hi. Bingley's friend Julie?"

"Yep! I just came from the airport."

"Oh. Where are you from?"

"Nebraska."

"Oh. Are you . . . um . . . just Bingley's friend?"

"Yes," I answered slowly.

She hadn't let me in yet. What did I have to do to get out of the North Carolina humidity?

"Oh. Because Wickham has a friend named Julie."

Being the wordsmith I am, I found her use of the present tense quite interesting. Wickham has a friend named Julie. I rolled this around in my head for a second, and then answered, "Really?"

Still standing on the porch, I endured a long awkward pause, and finally said, "Well, I used to be pretty close to Wickham. I just haven't talked to him in a while. Who are you?"

"I'm Lydia. Wickham's wife. I'm sorry, come in, come in!"

It was her, the girl Wickham brought with him when he visited me after my car accident. Her hair was shorter, but she was just as thin and just as quiet and just as plain. I looked around Bingley's house at pictures and books and movies, while she watched me.

"So, where are the boys?" I finally asked.

"Running errands. They should be back soon," she said.

"Ah." I lack the figurative language necessary to effectively describe how uncomfortable I felt in that house with that woman. But it was tangible. We flashed nervous smiles at each other  while I feigned concentration on Bingley's movie collection—which lacked the John Hughes canon and any Jane Austen adaptations. I tried, lamely, to engage her in conversation, but neither of us seemed to get past the awkwardness to say much of anything.

Bingley and Wickham didn't return for three days!

Okay, it wasn't three days. Lydia and I were alone for maybe 15 minutes, but the discomfort was so great that

I was in the process of locating the nearest exit when the boys walked in from the garage. Bingley gave me a hug, and then, strangely, so did Wickham. What floored me most was what Wickham said next: "You look really great!"

Bingley echoed him, to which I responded, "Ah, it's all smoke and mirrors, tanning and bronzer."

Wickham laughed.

I could still make him laugh. My heart fluttered a bit, then sank as I realized it didn't matter if I could make him laugh. That wasn't my job anymore.

The wedding party met at the house to caravan to the chapel. Since my hotel was close to the chapel, I wanted to drive instead of ride with someone. So I headed to my car, and Bingley's old roommate Trent said he'd ride with me so I wouldn't have to ride alone. I started to shrug him off, because I had to call someone, anyone, and replay the encounter with Wickham's wife. But Trent was insistent, so I caved.

Trent is a trip. Most of his stories begin with "We were so drunk" or "I was so hungover" and I always find stories like his entertaining, since I don't drink. What I really admired about Trent was that he simply lived his life and didn't much care about anything else. He was happy working at Costco, going fishing, golfing, drinking, and embarking on the occasional vacation. He was a welcome oasis during that drive, and talking with him was much better conversation than calling Deanne and rehashing the awkward encounter with Wickham's wife, which I would've done if I drove by myself.

We arrived at the church, and I saw Bingley's parents. Hope and Harry are my second set of parents. Sometimes, I take their advice over my own parents'. I've called them "Mom and Dad" since high school and every year, they send me a birthday card in the mail and sign it "Mom and Dad." They both squeezed the life out of me, and consequently, I started to cry. I passed off this initial emotional outburst as tears of joy in seeing Mom and Dad for the first time in three years. But as Mom held me, I wanted to break down completely and mourn Wickham. Again. Like I hadn't spent the better part of 10 years of my life mourning him.

Mom introduced me to her daughters and sons I had never met, and then she whispered, "Have you met Wickham's wife?"

I nodded as my eyes started to burn, and she asked, "How are you doing with that?"

A couple tears escaped and she squeezed my hand. A few tears fell from her eyes as well. She had watched Wickham and me dance around each other for a decade. She was Bingley's mom, but she was also my "mom" and Wickham's "mom," and when any of us hurt, she hurt too.

I made it through the rehearsal and the dinner with no major breakdowns. In retrospect, maybe I should have broken down that first day. Maybe it would have prevented what happened the next day. The wedding day.

Bingley called me early that morning to see if I'd like to run errands with him. As it would be the only time

I'd have alone with him, I readily accepted. We kept conversation light, and I allowed myself to bask in, and be in awe of, our relationship. Fifteen years we had been friends, and every time we got together, we picked up as if distance was never an issue. It amazes me still. Once he was done with his errands, we decided to see Mom and Dad at their hotel.

Bingley could've taken any number of family members or even Wickham out on his errands, but he made sure it was me. I was still important enough to him, and it filled me with pride. I don't remember what we were talking about, but I remember laughing as we pulled into a parking space, and I felt confident, special. And then I saw them.

Wickham and his wife were in the hotel's outdoor pool, tossing their toddler in the air between them. Their daughter shrieked with delight as she landed, splashing water on her parents. All three laughed. All three looked happy. All three made my stomach lurch, my head spin, and my eyes water.

Me, my brain screamed. That is supposed to be me.

I watched Wickham simultaneously rough-house and care for his daughter. His love for her was evident in every giggle and shriek that echoed across the pool. I watched his wife smile demurely as her husband played the appropriate role of "fun dad," and the scar tissue that had built up over heartbreaking years loving Wickham began to split wide open. I lowered my head as we walked toward the pool deck, took deep breaths, and put on my game face.

Mom and Dad sat on pool chairs, teasing their grandkids, while Bingley's sisters wrangled the other children. I disengaged for a moment to survey my surroundings. I would never have this: the cousins, the laughing, the grandkids, the kids. The scene before me might as well have been science fiction, a curious case study in a family structure I would never know.

I snapped back to my surroundings just as everyone decided it was time to clean up and get lunch so we could make it to the church in time for pictures. Bingley's sister, Caroline, invited me to wait in her room. I told her I'd just wait in the lobby, but her Southern charm would hear nothing of it, so I meekly followed.

Once there, she asked some basic get-to-know-you questions about what I'd been up to since high school, but then the million dollar question came: "Did any of y'all ever hook up?"

I had two obvious choices. I could lie and say no and avoid a messy display of emotion, or I could let the dam burst wide and tell her the truth. I decided I was strong, I could hold myself together, and told her that indeed, Wickham and I tried occasionally to have a relationship. "Oh. Then this must be kind of hard for you," she replied.

That's when it happened. I pride myself on keeping my emotions in check around strangers. For the most part, I can control my tears with a deep breath or a thought about something neutral. Something like pears. Or ducks. Alas, fruit and water fowl did not help me this day. Composure flew out the window, and I began to weep. Caroline was understanding and empathetic, and even went so far as to say she thought I could do much better than Wickham. All of this was intended to make me feel better, as it has been every time a boy breaks my heart. What else are people supposed to say? I couldn't fault Caroline for offering the same platitudes I'm always offered. Trouble is, those platitudes are cold comfort. I didn't feel better. I felt embarrassed that I told her, mortified at my emotional outburst.

Later that day as I milled around the chapel waiting for the wedding to begin, I was surprised by how hurt I felt, seeing Wickham with his family. I had no idea that they'd had a daughter, and seeing him hold his little 2-year-old's hand as she toddled across the campus grasses devastated me. I played nice and saved other emotional meltdowns for the privacy of my rental car or hotel room, but I've wondered since if he could see through my huge smile to what I was really feeling. After all, he was Wickham, one of the few people in my life who has known me for decades, and has seen all my dimensions.

Then again, he had changed.

At the reception, Bingley arranged for one of his very attractive groomsmen to dance with me as much as I wanted. It was sublime, and the endorphins made me feel invincible. During a dance break, I sauntered over to a table where Wickham and his wife were sitting. Nelly blared through the speakers, so I shouted, "Are you having fun?"

His wife curtly nodded and said, "This really isn't my

kind of music."

Wickham said, "It's getting hot in here,"

"So take off your clothes!" I said. This, to me, was an obvious nod to the rapper Nelly's song "Hot in Herre." Wickham used to know everything about music; I thought for sure he'd get the reference. What I saw instead were two horrified faces staring at me.

"You know, the song? By Nelly?" I said.

"Like I said, this really isn't my kind of music," his wife said.

"Yeah, we don't really listen to popular music that much," added Wickham.

Wickham—the guy who introduced me to Morrissey, The Smiths, Elvis Costello, Harry Connick, Jr. The guy who left three giant boxes of cassette tapes with me when he was on his mission because he wanted someone to listen to them while he was gone. The guy who had Nirvana and Primus and The Cure and Depeche Mode couldn't tell me who Nelly was?

"Want to get a drink?" Wickham asked.

"Sure," I said, and we walked over to the bar to grab water for him and a diet Coke for me.

"You really don't listen to music?" I asked.

"Not really. She doesn't like my music," he said.

We stood near the bar for a few minutes, making small talk. When we returned to the table, his wife decided she'd had enough Nelly—and by that time OutKast was also in heavy rotation—so it was time to leave.

"If you're ever in Idaho, you should come see us," she said.

"Thanks. I'll do that," I replied, knowing it would never happen. I had never had a reason to go to Idaho before, and couldn't imagine any scenario in which I'd make a special trip just to spend time with them.

I didn't talk to Wickham after that wedding. He had a life that really didn't have space for me, and I wasn't sure I wanted to be included anyway. Bingley was different; we were always friends. Wickham . . . Wickham was my Achilles Heel. I couldn't quite let him go, but keeping him close wasn't an option, either. Google made it easy to keep tabs on him, as he started a career in journalism. And in 2007, Google made it easy for me to reconnect with him.

# Reconnect/Disconnect

A story about his son, barely a year old and fighting cancer, was in the local paper he wrote for. His son, Sebastian, was awaiting live-saving medical treatment. I felt hollow as I read the story. I had known Wickham for almost 20 years, and this huge event in his life had to be weighing on him. So I swallowed my pride and wrote him a letter. Handwritten, sent to his home via snail mail, an apology for being absent in his life, I offered prayers for his son, and an invitation to talk if he ever needed to. Wickham called me the day he received the letter.

There was no awkwardness as we talked. It wasn't a long conversation, but we reconnected, and he sounded happy. I couldn't remember hearing him sound as happy as he did that day. And I know it wasn't about me—he had changed. The emo-boy-dressed-in-jock-clothing was now a father of two, and not just that, he was the father of a very sick little boy.

"I've actually been thinking about you a lot lately," he admitted.

"Really?" I said.

"We must be in tune with each other, because your letter arrived during the week when I was trying to figure out how to talk to you again," he said.

My heart smarted a bit at that remark, a reminder that we had an indelible connection, a connection that perhaps he lacked with his wife. I told him about grad school and life in Ohio, and he told me about life as a journalist and the steps that were being taken to save his son's life. When we hung up, I felt relief. I felt comfort.

Two months later, five days before I was supposed to drive to North Carolina to see Bingley and his wife, Bingley called me.

"Jules?" he said, his voice breaking.

"Bingley, what's wrong?"

"Sebastian died this morning."

Bingley went to the funeral, but plane tickets to Montana were expensive and I was a struggling grad student. I couldn't go. But I console with food. I made cookies and picked up some gift cards to Papa John's and mailed a package to Wickham and his grieving family. I felt helpless. The morning of Sebastian's funeral, as I was getting ready to go hiking to take my mind off the fact that I couldn't be there, my phone rang.

"Hey, Julie, it's Wickham."

As soon as I said hi, my voice broke, and I started to cry.

"I just wanted to thank you for the package you sent," he said.

"I'm so sorry I can't be there," I said.

"It's okay, it's okay."

"I am going to try to come visit this fall, I promise," I said. "Is the funeral already over?"

"No, we're starting in about an hour, but I just wanted to call. I'll admit, I was holding out hope that you'd show up and surprise me."

"I'm sorry. I wish I could be there," I said.

We stammered through the awkwardness that accompanies grievers and consolers, and said our goodbyes. Four months later, I did make that fall trip to see him and his wife and daughter. After a dinner with Bingley's parents, Wickham's wife took me aside.

"Thank you so much for coming. He's been so happy this week," she said.

"Oh, that doesn't have anything to do with me," I said.

"Not true," she said. "The only people he cares about more than me and Molly are you and Bingley."

I didn't know how to react to that.

Wickham and I talk once or twice a year now, and it's always good to hear his voice. There is always a part of me that will belong to him, whether he knows it or not. One time he called me on a day I was sure I had ruined a fledgling relationship. I mentioned as much to him. Wickham said he couldn't imagine someone not being crazy about me.

If only he had been crazy about me . . .

Maybe my sense of style was a little off, like Duckie's. Maybe I was too intense in my devotion to Wickham, like Duckie was to Andie. Or maybe John Hughes was just writing a movie and I shouldn't have allowed it to influence my relationship expectations. Either way, when Wickham appears in my Facebook news feed, my heart jumps a little, and then almost immediately it breaks a little, when I remember he's not mine at all, and no matter how many times I tell people he's one of my best friends, he's really not anymore.

July 8, 1984                                    p12

On this page, On page nine I had a list of girls
On this page, I'm doing boys and girl

Girls                          Boys
Annaka Leigh                   Andrew Tyler
Brenda Kay                     Brian ~~Mark~~ Mark
Collen Marie                   Cory Mark
Deidre Kathleen                David Wayd
Erica Marie                    Eric Jon
Francis Katie                  Frank Lee
Garnet Kathleen                Grant Jon
Helen Kay                      Herbert Mark
Iris Mae                       ~~Ian Mark~~
JoEllen                        Jonathan Wayd
Kathleen Tai                   Kyle Lowell
Laura Josephine                Larry Mark
Marlene Kay                    Mark Jonathan
Nancy Marie                    Nathan Joseph
Opal Lyn                       Paul Scott
Pamela Tai                     Quincy Lyn
Rebekah Leigh                  Richard Mark
Stephanie Dianne               Scott Mark
Tara Mae                       Tomas Scott
Ursula Mae                     Victor Mark
Veronica Leigh                 Zachary Jon
Wanda Kay
Xandra ~~E~~ Kay
Yvonne Marie

An alphabetical listing of possible baby names,
created when I was 11 years old.

# Plan C

Upon graduating from high school, I figured my life would end up in one of the following ways:

Plan A:
Go to BYU
Meet husband and marry at 21
Maybe graduate from college
Have first baby at 23
Have second baby at 25
Have third baby at 27
Have fourth baby at 29
Have twins at 31
Raise kids, run household, and live long happy life with husband

Plan B:
Go to BYU
Go on an LDS mission at 21
Marry at 23
Maybe graduate from college
Have first baby at 25
Have second baby at 27
Have third baby at 29
Have fourth baby at 31
Raise kids, run household and live long happy life with husband

That was it. My prospective life when I graduated from high school. By the end of my first full year of college, the only thing that changed was the 'maybe' graduate from college to 'definitely will' graduate from college. I still fully expected the marriage and kids package deal—like it was something I could pick up at Target. Instead, The Plan, in reality, looks like this:

Plan C
Go to BYU
Meet fiance, leave BYU and begin destructive path for a year
Wake up and leave the fiance, move in with parents
Sit on couch in depressive funk for eight months
Start college at local commuter campus
Get life together and go on mission
Survive three horrid heartbreaks
Graduate from college
Teach high school English
Go to grad school, write thesis
Return to teaching high school
Go on lots of first dates

My life has not, in any form, resembled the plans I'd made when I was a college freshman. While my "engagement" at age five was cute and silly, the second engagement was much less silly. I wanted to be with a Blaine or a Lloyd Dobler. Instead, I was with a combination of Stef from *Pretty in Pink* and Hardy from *Some Kind of Wonderful*, mixed in with a dash of

Leatherface from *Texas Chainsaw Massacre*.

I knew John Thorpe in high school, and after my sophomore year at BYU, when I came home for the summer, we started dating. Wickham was on his LDS mission, and Bingley had National Guard training most of the summer. I also dated two other boys at the same time, but after a month, it was John who made me choose. John was a foot taller than me with a lanky but muscular frame, crystal-blue eyes and blond hair styled in the popular skateboarded "flop" of the early 1990s. His go-to wardrobe consisted of shorts, a t-shirt and a flannel shirt—the Seattle SubPop uniform. He marinated in Aramis cologne—another significant departure from my usual desirables. I always preferred a soapy, laundered scent to my men. Not a fierce chemical enhancement intended to disguise what a shower and clean clothes could handle just fine. Come to think of it, the Aramis overuse was probably the first red flag.

He took me to see *Jurassic Park*—not a movie I really wanted to see—but it was time spent with him, so I tolerated the dinosaurs and when the lights came up, I realized from the crowd what a big deal the movie was. People swarmed around us, and we were nearly separated when he grabbed my hand, looked in my eyes and said, "I'm not losing you."

I was hooked.

*Jurassic Park* wasn't the only time John made me feel like I mattered though. I worked at Taco Bell that summer, and most days at the end of my shift, I found notes on my car, or sometimes even John himself would be leaning against my wood-paneled station wagon. He'd greet me with a hug and a kiss, and we'd be off for the evening. We had fun, but he wasn't Mormon, and that was a bit of a deal breaker. Even though I enjoyed my time with him, and he made me feel unlike any other boy had ever made me feel, I didn't want to love him, lest it lead to a non-LDS marriage.

This mindset proved to be problematic one hot July evening. We stood at his car outside my house, saying goodbye. And instead he said, "We have to talk."

Typically the harbinger of relationship doom, I narrowed my eyes. He was a great distraction from the lack of my dating success at BYU, and I wasn't ready to stop having built-in plans every night. The newfound exclusivity with him was reassuring. I knew who I'd go out with on the weekends; I had a concrete last call of the day. So when he began this conversation with such a clichéd breakup phrase, I flinched.

"I keep thinking about all these things going on all over the world, and how we never really know what is going on where and why does what we do even matter to anyone else, and you're going to Canada tomorrow--"

"Wait. Are you mad that I'm going to Canada with Aimee and Nikki?"

My roommates from BYU and I were heading to Cardston, Alberta for a friend's mission farewell. Even though the boy in front of me wasn't LDS, he wasn't initially upset with my planned weekend trip with my friends, so I was confused. He wasn't making any sense. He took a deep breath.

"No, no, I don't care that you're going to Canada. I don't know how else to say this. I love you."

I didn't know what to do. No one had ever said that to me before. And after only six weeks of exclusive dating, how could he know he loved me? It took me three years and two breakups with Wickham before I admitted I loved him—and I only admitted that to myself, not to him.

I knew I didn't love him. But I was too young and insecure to know that I could have told him that. And then there was the thought of two more years at BYU with very little dating success, watching roommates date and marry and date and marry . . . and this boy in front of me was telling me he loved me.

I should have just given him a hug. I could have even just kissed him. Or even smiled coyly and buried my head in his chest.

Instead, I heard myself say, "I love you too."

A friend once asked me if I could pinpoint a moment that changed the course of my life. For some it might be not taking a job, selecting a different college, or missing a train. For me, it was a starry, starry night in July, telling John that I loved him. This wasn't how I imagined my first "I love you." We weren't at prom, we hadn't just had sex, we weren't in the middle of a fight. I wore a non-descript T-shirt, soccer shorts, and Teva sandals. While Montana isn't humid, I was still sweaty from that evening's bike ride, and Vegas odds are that I hadn't even shaved my legs that day. My hair was barely still in a ponytail, and my makeup was long gone. This wasn't like the movies told me it would be. It was all wrong. My lack of makeup, my outfit, my response—I deviated from the script that Cameron Crowe and John Hughes had written for me—and that moment of dishonesty changed my life.

He was thrilled with my response, I pretended to be, and at the end of the summer I went back to BYU to start my junior year of college, convincing myself I was in love with this non-LDS boy. And he was a smooooooth talker. So romantic. This was before email, and he wrote me a letter every day filled with declarations of love and loyalty. The letters were numbered in the bottom right corner on the back of the envelope. And since the post office didn't deliver mail on Sunday, I received two letters on Tuesdays, because he still wrote one on Sunday. Not wanting to skimp on his love for me, he even sent Sunday's letter in a separate envelope with its own postage. He begged me to leave BYU and be with him in Montana. Since no boys at BYU were interested in dating me, I decided a non-LDS boy in the hand was worth any number of LDS boys in the bush. I dropped out of BYU in December and moved back to Montana. My parents were disappointed and distraught, but not angry. This wasn't the future they'd envisioned for me.

He officially proposed, tiny ring and all, on Christmas Eve. My mother was devastated. She had worked so hard to raise all of us to not marry outside the faith, and now her oldest was going to do just that. Additionally, my dad had military orders back to Nebraska at the end of January and I wasn't going to go with the family. John and I planned on a January 15 wedding at the courthouse, so we printed up invitations on my parents' computer and mailed them to friends and family. Then, a week before the wedding, John panicked and convinced me we should just live together for a while. So we set a June wedding date instead, and I moved my things into his tiny basement studio apartment.

The first time he hit me was the day my family left for Nebraska.

January in Montana is bleak—gray skies, brown grasses peeking out through random patches of snow, gusts of wind that make hair maintenance irrelevant, and temperatures that require a complete sacrifice of fashion sense. Even bleaker that January was watching my family drive south on Montana Route 200 from the side view mirror, as John and I drove north toward our apartment. I cried. I kept crying. I couldn't stop.

Five minutes into the drive, he said, "I don't get why you're crying. We get to be together now. Just us."

"I know, I know. I just know that I'll miss them. I love my family," I said through the sobs.

We drove another five minutes in silence. I stared out the passenger side window and wiped away the tears as they fell. I heard John sigh heavily. It made me cry more. The words stuck in my throat: Turn around. Speed. Catch up to my family so I can go with them. But my pride and fear of dying alone shoved them down. We arrived home, and trudged through the cold into the dimly lit basement studio apartment.

I took off my coat, still teary-eyed.

I hung up my coat and turned around to see John's

glowering face.

He grabbed me.

Hard.

"Stop. Crying. There's no reason for you to cry," he said, as his fingers dug into my arms, just below my shoulders.

I was shocked—he had never spoken to me this way, and certainly had never touched me like that before. I tried to back away, but his grip tightened.

"I'm serious. Stop crying." He shoved me with such force that I landed about three feet away, through the open bathroom door, hitting my head on the tile. I tried to get up. I looked at him, and red flags from the previous five months bombarded my brain. Forcing me to choose between him and the other guys I was dating was suddenly not sweet, it was possessive. Picking me up from work was suddenly not thoughtful, it was controlling. And then there was the phone call.

Three weeks before John and I were supposed to get married, my dad received a phone call at work. The caller refused to identify himself, but according to my dad, he shared sobering information.

"He said 'You cannot let your daughter marry John,'" my dad told me the night of the call.

"What? Who was this? Why?" I demanded.

My dad held up his hand to quell my defensive questioning. "I don't know who it was. And I hesitate to place any value in anonymous phone calls. If someone isn't willing to put his name behind something, I question the information. But this man sounded genuinely concerned, which is why I'm sharing it with you."

Sighing, I crossed my arms and cocked my hip. "Okay, then, what did he say?"

"He said that he's seen John become very violent. That one night in his basement he had a gun and talked about killing his mother. That John is very quick to get angry with people and run out of their lives."

I laughed. "That's absurd. John wouldn't hurt a fly."

As much as I knew my dad didn't like John, I could tell he didn't want to push me further away from the family. For a moment, it actually felt like my dad was on my side. His gentle delivery of this news, his suspicion of the caller's motives, it pointed toward a movement of endorsing my relationship with John. But three weeks later, lying on the bathroom floor, nursing a throbbing head, I realized both my dad and I had been duped. John stood at the bathroom door, a look of shock on his face.

"I'm so sorry," he said, and he rushed to me and helped me up. He kissed my forehead, stroked my hair, wrapped his arms around me and kept whispering, "I'm so sorry. Please don't leave. I'm so sorry."

"I'm fine. Don't worry about it," I said, and I looked up at him and kissed him.

It only got worse from there.

Not only was he physically abusive on a regular basis, he was controlling: I had no keys to our apartment, he wouldn't put me on his car insurance so I couldn't drive, and the money I earned from my dumb part-time job selling newspaper subscriptions went straight into the joint checking account we set up after we got engaged. He was suspicious: I once went to a movie with a girlfriend and when I came home, he was convinced I had hooked up with other guys while out. He was horribly mean. It's the only time in my life that I have no journal entries, because he thought it was stupid for me to write. He saw no need for me to finish college, even though I wanted to.

I never could tell what might trigger his outbursts. One time, I read a letter from a male friend, who was serving an LDS mission. After I read the letter, John was positive he saw me put the letter to my face in a longing way, as if to say I longed to be with this friend.

"Give me that letter," he said.

"Okay," I said, a little confused that he would want to read it since he wasn't a fan of LDS theology.

He ripped the letter into tiny pieces, eyes fixed on me the entire time.

"Why did you do that?" I asked, holding back tears that would surely ignite his already short fuse.

"You don't need to hear from him anymore. If he writes you again, you're not reading his letters," he replied coolly.

Sure enough, when another letter arrived, John ripped it in half, threw it in the garbage, and spit on it.

I spent a month treading softly and never knowing what might anger him, and after a screaming match in the local mall parking lot, I packed my belongings, carted them all to Bingley's house to stay with his parents, called my dad to come get me, and tried to hide out until my dad could get back to Montana. But John knew where I was and he showed up the next day. He came over while Bingley's parents were at work. I cracked the door open to see John shivering in the dreary February cold, head hanging, holding a bouquet of flowers in his hands. I propped open the storm door with my foot and looked at the top of his blond head.

"What do you want?" I asked.

He lifted his face, his mournful, sad, lying face, and said, "You. I need you. Please come home. I'm so sorry. It won't happen again."

"You say that now . . ." I started.

"I'm serious. I'm so sorry. I love you. I want to marry you and I want you to have my babies," he said.

With his free hand, he reached for my face. I backed away. The raging feminist in me was screaming to send him away. The terrified, helpless idiot in me believed every lie he spouted.

"Just let me come in and we can talk. Please. We'll just talk," he said.

And his mea culpa, combined with his sorrowful voice and, of course, the flowers, melted my pathetic, lonely heart and I let him in.

This is one place where the Lifetime Movie Network gets it right. I'd leave. Stay with Bingley's parents. Call my dad to see if he could arrange to come get me. Less than 24 hours later, John would be at the door or on the phone, sobbing, apologizing, promising to change, telling me he loved me. And every time, I believed him. So I'd go back. Three times, between February and April, the same cycle.

Since he wouldn't let me drive, he picked me up from work every night at nine. And he could be unabashedly romantic. On Valentine's Day, just one week after I tried to leave him the first time, when I walked out to the parking lot where he would be waiting, he was standing in front of his car, holding a boombox over his head, blasting "In Your Eyes" by Peter Gabriel. Sure, completely unoriginal since John Cusack did it in *Say Anything*, but John knew how much I loved that movie. Even though he woke up at 2 a.m. for his job at a local bakery, that night, he stayed up late. We drove to a hill where we could see the whole city. It was a relatively mild evening by Montana winter standards, so we sat on a bench, held hands and looked at the lights. He gave me flowers. When we finally got home, he asked me to get him some water. I opened the refrigerator, and there was a heart-shaped cheesecake with a note on it: I love you. Happy Valentine's Day. Days like these were rare, but they were enough to make me stay.

Plus, aside from the abuse, I loved our simple life together. We didn't have much money, so we played board games and cards. Occasionally we'd splurge on a movie and after one particularly brutal altercation, he took me to the symphony. I loved cooking for him, taking care of him when he was tired or sick. In short, it was the closest I'd been to being a wife and I loved the sense of purpose and fulfillment it gave me. If it meant enduring name-calling or the occasional beating, then that was the trade-off I had to be willing to make. Marriage, according to Jane Austen and my church, was the sole purpose of my existence, and I knew I could make this work. I knew I could.

One day in March, John came home from work around 7 a.m. I don't remember what made him so angry that morning, but when his temper was riled up, it was best to lie low and pray for it to blow over. It wasn't blowing anywhere that morning. He slammed his keys down on his desk. He threw his coat on the floor. He plopped onto the air mattress that was our bed. I lay still, eyes closed, though my mind was wide awake. Suddenly, he began kicking at my legs with enough force to push me off the mattress.

"Get up," he said.

I pulled my legs into a fetal position and tried to stay sleeping—as if playing possum was going to make this predator go away. He kicked my legs harder, at a more frenetic pace.

"I said, GET UP!"

The small apartment offered no place to hide. I rolled off the mattress to the hardwood floor. I tried to stand, but the force of his kicks stung my weakened legs.

"What? What did I do?" I asked, trying not to cry.

"You know what you did," he snarled, and he walked across the mattress toward me.

I scampered into the kitchen and slumped against the wall, in a tiny space between the stove and the refrigerator. He followed me. He was a foot taller than me, but as I cowered in a corner and he sized up all his height, he morphed into a barricade that I dare not try to breach. He pulled me up by my arms with such force that days later my triceps were still bruised. He shook me violently.

"You are worthless. No one will ever want you. I don't even want you," he said, as he pulled back his right arm. I could see it happening. Everything was simultaneously happening fast, yet in slow motion. I couldn't believe it. I watched his hand form into a fist, My brain didn't even tell my head to duck, as if it knew the blow was inevitable. If you've never been punched in the face before, it's a strange feeling. There's the moment of contact that's confusing and shocking. There's the next second when the brain starts communicating to the rest of the body what just happened. Pain receptors kick in, coupled with a little bit of shock, and then the brain tells you what to do: Run. Hide. Avoid. It took a second for my brain to tell me, "Oh that's right, you're in a studio apartment with no emergency exits and a very strong 6-foot, 2-inch man standing in front of you, and he just punched you in the eye."

This is when my brain told me, "Say nothing. Stop crying and maybe he'll stop."

And I sank to the floor.

"You're pathetic," he said as he spat at me, grabbed my left hand and tore the puny engagement ring from it with such force that he almost dislocated my finger.

He turned and left the kitchen. I heard him plop down on the mattress and pull the covers up. He tossed and turned a couple of times while I sat in the kitchen, sobbing silently. Eventually, the tears stopped. I looked at the dingy kitchen floor, a black and white diamond linoleum that refused to sparkle despite mopping twice a week. Maybe if I could find a way to make that floor really shine, then he'd be happy. My eyes moved to the tiny window just across from the sink. Since we lived in the basement, a terminal film of dirt covered the outside of the window. It would be easy enough to wipe it down once a week and maybe a little more light would get through and then he'd be happy. I looked at the two feet of counter space, the scratched up white cupboards and thought, "If I could just make this place look like it isn't a basement studio apartment we're renting for $300 a month, then maybe he'd be happy."

Maybe he would be happy. My happiness didn't matter. It wasn't my job to be happy in this, or any relationship. It was my job to make it work. Intended or not, that was the message I got from 19 years of lessons at church. A man's job was to provide, and John was doing that. He found the apartment, he had the apprenticeship as a baker, had a car. A woman's job was to make sure the man was happy. The right cross to my face was simply his way of telling me he wasn't happy. So it was my job to figure out how to fix it.

But in a rare moment of clarity I thought maybe I should first figure out if I wanted to fix it. What happened to me that I would tolerate this kind of treatment? How did I become a statistic? But most chilling—at what point would he actually kill me?

I didn't hear much movement after a while, and I crawled to the threshold where the kitchen and living room met. It still hurt to walk, and by this time, my face was throbbing from his punch. I peeked around the corner, and there he was, sacked out on the air mattress. I crept past him on trembling legs, hoping I wouldn't wake him, went into the bathroom and quietly shut the door. I looked in the mirror and could already see my eye swelling.

My memory is sketchy after that. I don't remember how long he slept. I don't remember what I said to him when he woke up. I do remember that he looked at my face, saw the marks on my legs, which had started to bruise, and he cried. He hugged me as I stood lifeless. I did not hug back.

"We should call the police," he sobbed. "I'm so sorry."

And I couldn't. I couldn't do it. Not because I was afraid of what would happen to him, but because I didn't want anyone to know that I was so weak that I couldn't leave a man who was beating me.

Three days later we were at his parents' house, my black eye more purple than anything, and his mom looked at me suspiciously.

"What happened to your eye?"

"Oh, we were tickling each other and his elbow caught me at a bad angle," I said, as I laughed perhaps a little too nervously.

She narrowed her eyes and said, "One of these days I'm going to sit you on a stack of Bibles and make you tell me how many times he's hit you."

I knew her first husband had abused her—she was quite open about that. Maybe she knew her son had violent tendencies. Maybe her son and I didn't hide the savageness of our relationship as well as we'd thought. But when his mom said that to me, it was the first time I thought I had to leave him for good.

Through phone calls late at night, my sister figured out he'd been abusing me, and she told my parents. For months, my family prayed that I would find a way to leave for good. And one Sunday morning as I brushed my teeth, I looked in the mirror and didn't even know who I was anymore. My eyes were sad. I tried to smile, and I couldn't.

I walked out of the bathroom and took a deep breath.

"I have to leave."

"Where do you want to go?"

"No, I have to leave you," I said.

His nostrils flared and his cheeks flushed, and after a few seconds he said, "Fine. Was getting tired of you anyway. You have until 5 tonight and then I'll start throwing your crap on the lawn."

I called my dad and told him I was ready to come home. By this point, I had already called him on three separate occasions to ask if he could come get me, and I canceled the request all three times. What were the chances that he would even believe me this time? Unbeknownst to me at the time, thirty minutes later, he was on the road to Montana with a trailer hooked up to the minivan, ready to bring me home. He wasn't going to wait for me to change my mind again. Which I did. The next morning, John and I met at a park on the banks of the Missouri River. We walked along a path and talked.

"I just don't understand why you are doing this to us," he said.

"I think I just need some time and space, and I think you could use it too," I replied.

"But I love you. I want to marry you. I want you to have my babies," he said.

Those three verbs—love, marry, have my babies— these were the only three things I ever wanted in life. And here was a man practically begging to give them to me, and I was walking away from it. At the time, I felt like an idiot. What if there would be no one else? What would I do then?

John dropped me back at the friend's house where I was to wait for my dad (Bingley's parents were out of town, so I had to find a different safe house). I called home 24 hours after asking my dad to rescue me. Deanne answered the phone.

"Hi," I started.

"If you're calling to tell Dad not to come get you, it's too late. He's on his way."

"But John came over this morning and we talked, and I know it can be better. He wants to have kids right away. We'll be fine," I said.

"Like kids will make it better. That's nice. You're coming home," she said.

The next morning, my dad and I stopped at a grocery store on the way out of town to pick up some supplies. John was just getting off work and he saw the van and trailer in the parking lot. He pulled up next to the van, where I was sitting in the passenger seat. I didn't want to go into the grocery store; I was the kind of heartbroken that made it hurt to walk. John got out of his car, and I rolled down my window.

"You don't have to do this. You don't have to leave," he whispered, as he rested his head on the door.
I ran my fingers through his hair and kissed the top of his head. "I know. But I don't think my dad is going to give me a choice. I'll be back before the summer's over."

He lifted his head, opened the car door, took my hand and helped me stand. He brushed his hand alongside my cheek, then kissed me. We were still kissing when my dad returned to the van. My dad cleared his throat.

"Okay Julie, it's time to leave."

I hugged John as he said, "I'm going home right now and writing you a letter. It will be in Omaha by the time you get there."

That letter was there when I arrived in Omaha, in much better shape than I was. Angry at my sister for selling me out, angry at my dad for getting me, angry at both of my parents for not giving me driving privileges, I spent three weeks making plans to go back to Montana. By the fourth week home, I was in therapy, and by July, after several group and individual therapy sessions, I told him I was willing to come back if he would get help for his anger problems.

He called me all kinds of names, told me I was the one with the problem, and before he hung up, the last thing he said to me: "You will never find someone else who will want to marry you."

# Sweet Jane

I didn't grow up reading Jane Austen. It wasn't until my junior year of college, when I took a Jane Austen Seminar for one of my English Literature electives at the University of Nebraska-Omaha, that I knew she existed. On the first night of class, the teacher warned, "If you don't like marriage or have a hard time reading about relationships, you need to drop this class. Because that is all we talk about."

I was in the throes of a relationship with Mr. Knightley at the time, and I thought he would eventually propose, so I stayed in the class and read *Emma*, *Pride and Prejudice*, *Northanger Abbey*—all told, we read one Austen novel a week. That's a lot of tales of love, lots of weddings, lots of passionate speeches from men declaring undying love to ever-deserving female protagonists.

Knightley and I met 10 days after I came home from my mission. His mother dragged him to my sister's bridal shower for the sole purpose of meeting me, because my new mission (according to her) was to cure her son of his obsession with an undesirable mate and secure his eternal companionship for my own.

No pressure.

We began an electronic friendship—IMs and emails in AOL's heyday—and finally he asked me out on a date. We would see *Armageddon* (the movie, not the real event) and grab a bite, and see where the night took us. He lived an hour away, and I don't remember why I agreed to drive to him, but I did. I arrived at his house, his mother beaming, and we hopped in his Jeep and headed out.

At the first stop sign, my seat slid forward.

"Oh. Yeah, that seat is broken and doesn't hold its place. It's been a while since I've had any passengers. Sorry," he said.

So I braced myself, using my weight to try and hold the seat in place. Every stop sign and red light sent me toward the windshield; every acceleration sent me toward the backseat. He needed to get money for our date, so we went to the ATM, where he discovered his account was overdrawn.

"I have money," I offered.

"No, it's okay. I have some at home. We can go back and still make it in time," he said.

We arrived at his house, and I unbuckled my seat belt.

"No, stay in the car," he said, "I'll just be a minute."

"Okay," I said.

From the front seat of his Jeep, I watched as he asked his mom for date money. I felt bad, because I really am a low-maintenance date kind of girl. Hang out, play a board game, crack jokes with me, and I'm happy. But with money in hand, we proceeded to the theater. My friends at work had warned me that I would probably cry at the end of the movie, so I'd been steeling myself all day against any display of emotion. I hadn't cried on a first-date movie in seven years, and I didn't want to do it again. We sat through the slow motion, animal-cracker, save-the-world epic that is *Armageddon*, and I was strong. Not a glimmer of a tear. The credits rolled, and I looked at Knightley to ask how he liked the movie. He was a mess. He wiped away tears with his sleeve and I looked away. I was speechless. I'd been so focused on not crying myself that it never occurred to me that my date might cry. I swooned a little, and it really did endear him to me. I was hooked.

In hindsight, my relationship with Knightley was never solid. I can say now that I forced a lot of it. But he didn't exactly discourage me, either. He worked full time for an investment company in Lincoln in their IT division, and I was wrapping up courses before student teaching. Since my schedule was more flexible, I drove to Lincoln most weekends. I had other friends in Lincoln, too, and if I spent time with them without checking in with him, he would be disappointed. So I saw him quite often. His mother adored me, and she banked on me taking over their guest room every weekend. Early in our relationship, Wickham called and emailed me several times in a couple of days. I'd been avoiding the calls and not returning the emails. I told Knightley how hard it was for me to even fathom talking to Wickham.

"You just have to give it time," Knightley said.

"I just want to not feel anything at all," I said.

"That's not true. Emotions are good. It's what tells us we're alive," he said.

"I suppose," I said.

"Look, you'll get over him eventually. It just takes time. It took me a while, but I finally started getting over the last girl who broke my heart," he said.

"Really? When?" I asked.

"July," he said, and he smiled at me.

July is when we met.

Later that night after we had half-eaten our dinner, we drove out to the country. It was a perfect fall night: clear skies, bright stars, and a slight chill in the air. He found a place to pull over, and we got out of his Jeep and sat on the hood, looking up at the stars. I breathed in the sweet smell of freshly cut hay, closed my eyes, and memorized that moment. I felt so comfortable, so at home. I opened my eyes, and the first constellation I saw was Orion. I thought of Wickham and looked at Knightley. He was staring at the sky, looking deep in thought. He wasn't my typical type--my insecure body issues had me gravitating toward tall, dark, and somewhat handsome men. Knightley was short, with more delicate features, and, while cute, he wasn't conventionally handsome. But he had a great smile and a tender heart. That moment, sitting on the hood of his Jeep, I decided I would be more than happy to fall in love with him.

Not that he made it very easy.

Most of September, October, and November, Knightley kept me in a pretty decent state of what experts call "wound tight." Not really committing to me, but not wanting to let me go, Knightley would one day email me three times and IM with me for hours, then not talk to me for days, then want to see me on the weekends. It was horribly confusing. But the simulation of a boyfriend was better than none, plus when we did talk, it was the perfect combination of flirtation and interest. So I allowed the torture to continue. Whatever you would call us was convincing enough for those three months that his parents thought it would be a great idea if our families had Thanksgiving dinner together. So his mom, dad, and brother all drove to my parents' house for a joint Turkey dinner.

I was going to make it Custer's Last Stand.

Despite my relatively open-book face, I can transform into the iciest of ice queens when I want to. And I wanted to that day. I was tired of the inconsistencies in our budding relationship, and I thought if I froze him out, he would either leave me alone for good or realize he wanted to be with me. I was cordial, but not affable. I didn't really want any down time with Knightley around, so I set to doing the dishes not long after we finished eating. Knightley followed me into the kitchen.

"Are you okay?" he asked.

"Yep. I'm great," I said, scrubbing at a plate.

"Are you sure?" he asked again, and he touched the small of my back.

I didn't react positively to the affection, but instead moved closer to the sink, away from his hand.

"Yep. I'm super. Just want to get these dishes done."

"Can I help?" he asked.

"If you want. I don't care," I said.

And we stood there in silence for 20 minutes, washing,

rinsing, drying. He finally retreated to the couch and lay down. It was a nice day outside, so the parents decided on a walk, and our brothers were playing video games in the basement. I finished the dishes and walked into the family room where Knightley was resting. I sat down next to him, on the opposite end of the couch. He sat up and started rubbing my back.

"Are you going to tell me what's wrong?" he asked.

"I told you. I'm fine. Nothing is wrong," I said, flinching at his touch but also wanting to sink right into it.

"I don't believe you. You're not yourself. Why won't you talk to me?"

"What's the point?" I responded. I started to get up, and he pulled me next to him so I was lying down also. He draped his arm around my waist and rested his hand on my stomach. He tried tickling me.

"Stop. You're just trying to make me talk to you," I said, and I put my hand on top of his, flat. Yet he gently wove his fingers through mine. He nuzzled the back of my neck and whispered, "You make it hard for me to keep my hands to myself. And you smell amazing."

He wrapped his other arm around me, started to squeeze, and nuzzled even more. For five heavenly minutes, we lay on the couch spoon-style, saying nothing, our legs intertwined and our hands occasionally lightly squeezing each other. Then his family bounded up the stairs, and like shrapnel, we separated. He and his family left, and I was completely confused. What just happened? Why was he so handsy? Was he finally ready to start a real relationship and stop the inconsistent whatever-we-were doing? I wanted an answer. I was tired of the back and forth, of never knowing. Plus I was angry that he quite easily melted the ice queen facade I had kept up for most of Thanksgiving Day.

So the next night I drove to Lincoln. I knocked on the door. He answered.

"I feel like I'm being played," I said.

"Um," he said, and he shivered a little from the cold. "Do you want to come in?"

"Sure."

We sat at the breakfast bar. "Do you want to start that again?" he asked.

"Yes. I feel like I'm being played. I'm trying to figure out exactly what we are to each other. If we're just friends, then I definitely feel like I'm putting more into the friendship than you are. But I can't read your mind, so when you flirt with me, I don't know if friendship alone is your sole objective. And I just want to know. This is your opportunity to define the relationship. Whatever you say goes."

He was quiet for a long time. He looked at the floor and said, "I'm sorry about yesterday."

Never wanting to let people know I am capable of being hurt, I said, "That's okay. I figured it was mostly loneliness and hormones anyway."

*We interrupt this memoir for a special presentation, brought to you by all the makers of antidepressants.*

INTERLUDE:

An Imagining of How Knightley Would
Have Responded if John Hughes or
Cameron Crowe Were Writing My Life


Knightley
Loneliness and hormones? How could
you say that?


Julie
Well? You've been so inconsistent
with everything. You tell me I'm
important to you, you go through
phases of being physical with me,
yet I don't even know what to tell
people when they ask what you are
to me.


Knightley
I know I haven't been very upfront
with you. And I'm sorry for that.
I'm trying to figure out exactly how
to tell how I feel about you. You
don't make it easy. You're so smart,
and funny, and adorable. When I'm
with you, you make me feel like I
can do anything. I feel

proud. I feel like a man. Can't you see what you do to me? I'm aloof sometimes because I'm afraid you're going to realize what a fraud I am, and you'll just leave and break my heart.

Julie
(reaching out to touch his face)
Leave you? I could never leave you. I'm falling in love with you.

Knightley
(tears in his eyes)
You don't know how happy I am to hear you say that. Of course yesterday wasn't loneliness and hormones. I was trying to show you how I really feel about you. I'm falling in love with you too.

(Knightley takes Julie's face in his hands and kisses her. End Scene.)

*And now, back to our regularly scheduled self-indulgent memoir.*

"Yeah, that's about what it was," he said.

I knew he was going to agree with me, but the movie-script endings I had been raised with filled me with hope that he would actually engage in some version of the above imagining.

"Do you have any idea how that makes me feel? It makes me feel cheap, and used."

His eyes colored a little red, and he held my gaze for several seconds.

"Julie, despite my actions, I do value your friendship very much. You mean a lot to me. But beyond that—with anyone—I just don't know. I feel so lost when it comes to that."

"I know," I said.

We looked at each other a little longer, and then his parents and brother walked in with groceries. I was shaking all over. I had done it to myself. I asked him to define the relationship, and he did. Friends. Again. Duckie. I didn't want to lose it in front of his family, so I quickly grabbed my coat and purse and left. I cried for 45 miles.

However, apparently once you snuggle with me, it's impossible to stop thinking about me. We spent most of December with each other, and by Christmas the snuggling turned into full-on making out in private, hand-holding in public (even at church—and THAT is when you know something is for real). Just after New Years, we went to a job fair in Omaha and then back to my house for a nap. But while he slept, I thought. We hadn't ever officially declared ourselves as exclusive. If we were going to continue being so physical, I wanted to know. When it was time to wake him up, I stood next to him and shook his shoulder. He slowly opened his eyes, smiled, reached up his arm and held my hand and pulled me down to the couch, just like he had on Thanksgiving. We snuggled for a few minutes, and then I turned around to face him.

"What are we doing?" I asked.

"We should probably figure that out. Do you know what you want?" he asked.

"I think I do," I said.

"I'm planning to move to Utah at the end of the month, but now I'm not so sure. I'm open to suggestions. Even biased ones," he said.

I looked him straight in the eye and said, "Stay. Don't leave."

He kissed me more sweetly than he ever had before.

"I have to decide by the weekend. Will you come down to Lincoln this weekend?"

"Of course," I said.

"It could be a really good weekend," he said.

I went to Lincoln that weekend and we revisited our favorite haunts: Valentino's for dinner, where neither of us got our money's worth from the all-you-can-eat buffet; Homer's records, where I pored through The Smiths, The Cure, and Morrissey while he checked out the latest hip-hop and dance music; Barnes and Noble, where I took him by the hand to the children's section and read him the classic *Everybody Poops*.

We stopped at Village Inn for pie, we went to church,

and whenever I was within arms reach of him, he made sure we were connected. Hand-holding, arm draped around my shoulders, and plenty of passionate kisses.

Sunday after church and lunch, we lay on his bed to take a nap. He closed his eyes and I burrowed into the crook of his arm. I dreaded the conversation we were bound to have, and couldn't fall asleep—which had never happened before. Sunday afternoon naps had become routine, and once settled into each others' arms, it didn't take long to drift off. But that Sunday, he also struggled to sleep. Five minutes of trying to sleep, eyes still closed, he said, "Should we talk now?"

"Sure," I answered, and I sat up. He stayed lying down.

"I have to go to Utah," he said.

My head spun and I couldn't breathe.

"Why?" I asked.

"Because. I can't stay here. I have to prove to my parents that I can make a life for myself without their help. I have to prove it to myself. And it could end up being a complete failure, but I have to at least try. I have to," he said.

I didn't know what to say to that, and I could tell I wasn't going to change his mind. Besides, I didn't want to change his mind. I wanted him to choose me, not Utah. I managed a half-smile and said, "Okay. Well, I should go."

He tugged at my arm, tried to pull me into his chest, but I resisted.

"No, please. Stay. Let's talk," he said.

"I'm not sure I have anything to say. You're leaving. Are you changing your mind?"

"No," he sighed.

"Then what could we possibly have to talk about?" His face looked pained—a look I hadn't seen from him before, and frankly, it angered me. He was choosing this. He didn't have to look pained. He could stay, he could marry me, and that pained look could disappear.

"I'm going home," I said, and I got off the bed.

He stood and gave me a hug. His arms around me always felt normal, natural, as if they were an extension of my own body and belonged to me. I could do anything, say anything with those arms around me. Tears rolled out the corners of my eyes.

"I love you," I whispered into his shoulder.

"I know you do," he said.

I broke his hug, put on my coat, and drove home.

I hadn't been home long when the phone rang. It was Knightley.

"I wanted to make sure you got home okay," he said.

"Yeah, I did. I'm fine. Tired. Sad," I said.

"You know the only thing that's going to change is geography," he said. "Nothing else will. You and I are still us."

"Promise?" I said.

"Promise," he said.

Three weeks later, on a snowy January weekend, I watched him pack his things. We went to dinner and picked at our food, barely looked at each other, barely talked to each other. Saturday morning I woke up early, showered and dressed, kissed him goodbye.

"I'm not leaving for a couple of hours," he said, squeezing my hand.

"I can't watch you drive away. I'll never make it back to Bellevue," I said.

He nodded as his eyes watered. I reached my hand up to the side of his face, and stroked his cheekbone. Doing something with my hands made it easier to focus on not crying.

"I'll call you when I get to Utah," he said.

"Okay," I said.

He did call when he got to Utah, and he emailed, and we chatted occasionally. When he told me the only thing that would change between us was geography, I believed him. But when I visited him in March, it was clear that more than geography had changed.

I had a week off for spring break so naturally I spent it in Utah. I made plans to stay with Bex, a friend from my mission to Quebec. Knightley picked me up from the airport, but rather than park and meet me at the gate, he waited for me curbside. This, of course, occurred in the days when meeting someone at the gate was often a sign of how much people cared about each other. I picked up my parents from the airport dozens of times, and even though they often said, "Don't come to the gate," the subtext was always "But if you really love me, I'll see your face as soon as I step off the jetway."

Knightley seemed irritated when I hopped in his Jeep.

"Everything okay?" I asked.

"Just a long day at work. I'm tired," he said.

"Oh. Well. Uh...thanks for picking me up. I guess we don't have to go to dinner. You can just take me to Bex's house."

"No, no, it's okay. We can grab something to eat."

"No, if you don't want to go to dinner, then let's not go to dinner. I don't want you to be upset that I flew all the way out here and then just resent me through an entire meal," I snapped.

He sighed. I stared out the passenger side window. He didn't reach for my hand or my knee, and I chewed on my lip and focused on not crying. Geography was definitely not the only thing that had changed.

We ended up at Barnes and Noble that night with Bex, and I excused myself to the restroom. While I was gone, Bex—ever the protective friend—dug into him.

"So is Julie still your girlfriend?" she asked.

"No," he said.

"Is there someone else then?"

"Sort of," he said.

"Then you need to tell her. Don't give her false hope," Bex said.

"I know. I'm just scared," he said.

Because Bex could tell he wasn't interested in being all that forthcoming, she shared this conversation with me in her bedroom later that night.

"So you have a choice," she said. "You can wait and see if he will come clean, or you can start the conversation and make him come clean. Which one will make you feel better?"

I loathe confrontation, especially when confrontation

will seal my fate of dying alone. By the time my Utah trip rolled around, I had read *Sense and Sensibility* and *Pride and Prejudice* and I did not recall the women of Austen's novels actively calling out suitors who had fallen out of favor. Pine away? Yes. Fall on a fainting couch and lament her existence? Sure. Write longing letters to boon companions? Absolutely.

Knightley picked me up the next morning. We stayed silent as he drove up a canyon, the radio shuffling through bubblegum pop music. As we neared the pull off we had planned to visit, "The Hardest Thing" by 98 Degrees came on the radio. I laughed. Knightly flipped off the radio. He pulled into a parking spot at a trailhead, turned off the jeep, and put his head on the steering wheel.

Dramatic, much?

I couldn't take the silence, and it was clear he wasn't going to start the conversation, so it fell to me.

"So I feel a bit used and cheap again. Bex told me about your conversation last night. Why couldn't you have told me this before I came to Utah?"

Silence.

"I'm not even sure I want to be around you right now. You've slowly made yourself more and more inaccessible, instead of just telling me straight up you've moved on. Even though you told me geography was the only thing that would change. Two months ago, that's what you told me."

Silence.

"I'm not sure I can even trust you. I don't even feel

like your friend right now."

Silence.

And then, "I don't know what to say. Nothing I say would matter anyway if you don't trust me," he said.

"So you won't even try?" I asked.

"Look, I can really really like a girl, but in my heart, I want to feel like I can give her everything. I've only felt that way once and she didn't want it. I tried to get to that point with you, and maybe I'm trying too hard," he said.

"So what changed all of the sudden? For all of February, I really did feel like geography was the only thing that changed," I said.

"I gave up," he said.

I took a moment to process that admission. Noting that he still hadn't admitted he was kind of seeing someone else, I was more angry that he just gave up. Gave up on me. Gave up on us.

"You just gave up? You made a decision that affected me without even telling me?" I asked.

"I have this idea of how a guy should treat a woman and I can't live up to that right now. I don't know if I ever will," he said.

"I wish you could see what I see when I look at you. You are smart, intelligent and you have so many other qualities—" I started.

He interrupted. "I just don't see that."

"That's why we're not supposed to be alone, because we hardly see the good in ourselves, and other people can point it out to us," I said.

He took a deep breath.

"How long would you wait?" he asked.

"What? Wait for what? Wait for you?" I asked.

"Yes. How long would you wait for me to figure out my future?"

"A long time," I said.

"I know. And I can't let you pass up opportunities because I don't know if I'll ever get better," he said.

"What if you are my opportunity?" I asked.

"I don't feel like anyone's opportunity right now," he said, and his head went back to the steering wheel.

In retrospect, that was a lie. He clearly felt like someone's opportunity. Even though this self-esteem crisis may have been real, he still wasn't giving me the real reason why he bailed on me.

"Let me ask you this, then. The whole time we were together, did you ever think about what you said to me before you said it? Or think about your actions?"

"I tried to," he said.

"If you had no intention of getting serious with me, you should have told me," I said.

"I would have."

By the end of that trip up the canyon, the relationship was officially over, and I still had a month of this crappy Jane Austen class. The last book we read was *Persuasion*, and it ignited in me a new hope, a new kind of myth to believe in.

# Wentworth is Dead.

Prior to my first reading of *Persuasion*, all of Austen's books were somewhat indistinguishable from a John Hughes or Cameron Crowe movie. Initially mis-matched couple? Yep. Couple overcomes obstacles? Yep. Couple ends up together? Yep. Standard, standard, standard. But *Persuasion* is different. *Persuasion* is still the myth I buy into. It's not Austen's most famous piece, so for the uninitiated, here's a summation:

The Players: Anne, her father, Captain Wentworth, various and sundry haughty women consumed with marriage.

Anne, eight years prior to the novel's start: "Wentworth! I love you! But my father and aunt, who are convinced you will never amount to anything, don't want me to marry you. So I'm not going to, because this is Victorian England, so I do whatever the man in charge of me says."

Wentworth: "Aw, man! Even though I'm in the military and will have a steady income for the rest of my life? Oh well. Okay."

Anne, to herself: "I wonder why he didn't fight for me. Must not have really loved me. Sigh. I will die alone."

Eight years later . . . .

Anne: "Wow. The boys are back in town. Wentworth

is now a captain. And he's rich. And he's still hot. Oh, and I still love him, but I am plain, and I am 27 years old and therefore near-dead, and he will never want to be with me because I am near-dead, at 27 years old. I am going to die alone, a burden to my father and my married sisters. So I might as well head to Bath and spa it up for a couple of months. Oh, and it's clear Wentworth never really loved me anyway. Humph."

Wentworth: "Anne, how dare you accuse me of not loving you, or of not even missing you? I've loved you all of this time, and I KNEW your dad didn't think I was good enough, but I think you should tell your dad to shove it. I love you. Don't ever think that men love less than women or that men hurt less than women. I love you. Always have, always will."

Anne: "Okay then! I will buck all tradition of being obedient to my father and I will be with you!"

The actual letter from *Persuasion* in which Wentworth declares his love is so exquisite that I have it bookmarked and sometimes will read it and sigh and read it and sigh and read it . . . so please, read it and sigh with me:

> Anne,
> I can listen no longer in silence. I must speak to you by such means as are within my reach. You pierce my soul. I am half agony, half hope. Tell me not that I am too late, that such precious feelings are gone for ever. I offer myself to you again with a heart even more your own than when you

almost broke it, eight years and a half ago. Dare not say that man forgets sooner than woman, that his love has an earlier death. I have loved none but you. Unjust I may have been, weak and resentful I have been, but never inconstant. You alone have brought me to Bath. For you alone, I think and plan. Have you not seen this? Can you fail to have understood my wishes? I had not waited even these ten days, could I have read your feelings, as I think you must have penetrated mine. I can hardly write. I am every instant hearing something which overpowers me. You sink your voice, but I can distinguish the tones of that voice when they would be lost on others. Too good, too excellent creature! You do us justice, indeed. You do believe that there is true attachment and constancy among men. Believe it to be most fervent, most undeviating, in

F. W.

I must go, uncertain of my fate; but I shall return hither, or follow your party, as soon as possible. A word, a look, will be enough to decide whether I enter your father's house this evening or never.

I used to read that letter and wonder where the hell my Captain Wentworth is. Problem is my Captain Wentworth(s) are all married. I will get no heart-melting letter from someone I dated, because all the boys I've dated have wives and children. I can no longer rationally hope for a Captain Wentworth, because if someone from my past does happen to send me a letter declaring his undying love for me, it means he's either widowed or divorced, and I would never wish either unhappiness on any of my old boyfriends.

For a couple of years I thought that Knightley was my Wentworth. When I moved to Utah after graduating from college, he was still there, dating someone else. But he worked in Salt Lake and I lived in Salt Lake, so we would meet for lunch occasionally. He was the only guy I was ever able to cobble together a friendship with after dating seriously, and we really had the same connection as we did when we dated, minus the kissing and cuddling. One December day, he asked if I was free to run errands with him. He lived an hour away in Utah County, but he really wanted to see me, so I drove south to spend time with him. There was always the possibility that he was no longer with the girlfriend, and I didn't want to miss a chance to be with him if that was the case.

We met at a new mall in south Provo. I figured I'd be helping him pick out a new winter jacket or that the latest Robert Jordan book had been released.

(Side note: this was one thing that drove me absolutely insane about Knightley. He LOVED Robert Jordan. Jordan is a Tolkien wannabe—he created a world with all kinds of creatures and geographies that make no sense to me. I tried reading the first book in the 197 book series, and I wanted to gouge out my eyes. But I'm an equal opportunity hater. I feel the same way when forced to read Tolkien.)

As we walked through the mall and we passed the clothing stores and then the bookstores, I looked ahead to see where he might be going. Slowly, the gears clicked and I figured it out. Straight ahead of me was Fred Meyer Jewelers. Knightley changed course slightly and quickened his pace. That was indeed his destination. I stopped walking about 15 feet from the store. He turned around.

"Aren't you going to come with me?" he asked.

"Um, are you buying  ME  something in there?" I countered.

"No, I need to pick up Brittany's engagement ring," he said.

Now, if I had any modicum of chutzpah, I would have turned around and walked out of the mall. I was too shocked, too amazed that he would actually invite me to go with him to pick up the engagement ring for not me.

"I'll just wait in the food court," I said. He had promised me Panda Express if I took the time to be with him.

"No, just come in with me," he pleaded.

"Knightley, if I go in there with you, they will want me to try on the ring. They will assume I am your fiancée," I said.

Slowly, I watched the light bulb click on in his head. He hadn't considered that. As far as he was concerned, I was just his friend with him on an errand. I wasn't a girl, and definitely not The Girl. I sighed, headed toward the food court and waited.

Ten minutes later, he found me, little black box in his jacket pocket.

"Do you want to see it?" he asked.

Oh sure. I'm into this kind of torture, I thought.

"I don't care," I said, as he pulled it from his coat.

He opened the box. I can't remember what it looked like, only that it wasn't anything I would have wanted to wear.

He sat on that ring for two months before finally proposing to Brittany. Even though Knightley got engaged in February and was married in May, he still called me. Usually at odd times, and never with a real purpose other than "just to talk." One September night at 11:30 p.m., he called. He'd been married for two months.

"What do you want, Knightley?" I said with exasperation in my voice.

"I want to talk to you. I miss you," he said.

"You have a wife now. Talk to her. You can't call me anymore," I said.

I never heard from him again.

The last Wentworth was gone.

# Lloyd Dobler

I faced my dad's first cancer surgery without Tilney. We had barely met then, but by the time the doctors found that cancer had spread to my dad's liver, Tilney and I were quite serious.

I didn't want to date Tilney. Throughout the course of our eight-month relationship, my journal is littered with entries begging myself to just let him go. I knew he was going to break my heart.

*October 23, 1999*

*I just got home from an eight-hour date with Tilney. I need to stop seeing him. I try to keep telling myself he's young, he's leaving in two months, don't even bother. But he's nice and he's cute and we talk a lot. I don't want to like him. I want him to be boorish and repulsive. I just want him to be a jerk like all the others. My heart literally feels weak. I just can't take another one. I can't do it.*

*October 24, 1999*

*Keep thinking about last night . . . a big part of me really liked having someone with me. After so many months of going places alone, it was great to have someone intelligent around—I really just let him ramble an awful lot, but I liked hearing him talk. We went dancing, and I loved dancing with him. But I can't do this. Have to talk myself out of it. Have to. Can't do this. Just can't.*

This entry, written after my dad was diagnosed with liver cancer:

*November 10, 1999*
*Tilney and I went to the symphony and then he came over for ice cream. Lauren had told him about dad's cancer, and he tried to talk to me about it, but I didn't want to. Before he left, he was standing at the top of the steps outside, and I cracked some joke and said goodbye. He said, "Julie, is there anything I can do for you?" I wanted to say—just hold me, let me cry, listen to me— but I just fought back tears and said, "No. I'm fine."*

And then this one, after a month of dating him:

*November 14, 1999*
*I really don't want to spend time with Tilney—just because I enjoy being with him, and he's leaving, so really, what's the point? There isn't one. So if I stop now, I won't get attached. Then I won't get hurt.*

But at the same time I wrote these entries, I felt he was The One. John, Cameron, and Jane had been telling me for years that there was only One for me, and while I loved Wickham and Knightley, I felt an assurance with Tilney that I lacked with the others.

With all apologies to Chuck Klosterman, men alone cannot claim Lloyd Dobler ruined their relationships. Lloyd ruined women, too. Because after *Say Anything* hit movie theatres in 1988, every girl expected every boy to be Lloyd Dobler. Sweet, doting, sensitive and caring Lloyd. This is what we deserved! This is what we should wait for! And for a few months, Tilney was my Lloyd Dobler.

Tilney was my friend Lauren's brother. He was wrapping up his mission in Sweden when he wrote to her that he felt he should move to Omaha and live with her rather than heading home to Ohio. There may have been something in there about meeting his wife in Omaha, but that is urban legend. Since I never heard it first-hand, it's not my place to perpetuate that rumor. However, the events of September-December 1999 do a dang good job of corroborating that legend. (I'll take this opportunity to remind readers that 75% of what the National Enquirer reports is true, so rumor and innuendo actually do mean things. Sometimes. Oh, and I occasionally make up statistics to serve my own purposes).

Tilney was five years younger than me, which in Mormon years is actually five decades. I was nearing the end of my prime baby-making window, which made me an unsuitable wife candidate. So why spend time dating a younger man if he was just going to bail on me for a fertile 18 year-old who wanted a baker's dozen of children? Plus, I knew he would be heading to BYU in a matter of months, where the girl-boy ratio is two to one, and the girls there are much thinner and much prettier than me. But since all he did was work at Omaha Steaks, and all I was doing was working 30 hours a week, taking 17 credits, and watching my dad battle cancer, I suppose neither of us had anything better to do.

For our first official date, we attended a marching band competition at Memorial Stadium in Lincoln, Nebraska. Romantic, right? I was a youth adviser at church, and one of my girls was the drum major for a band so I told her I would see her perform. I drove Tilney to Lincoln to minimize the appearance of a date. When we arrived at the stadium, I grabbed a heavy blanket from my trunk.

"Let me carry that for you," he said.

"I can carry it myself. I don't need your help," I countered.

We were an hour away from home watching marching bands. In no world of Jane Austen, John Hughes, or Cameron Crowe was this a date.

We walked to the ticket office, and I pulled out my wallet as if it was high noon in New Mexico.

"Let me pay for you," he said.

"You don't have to. I can do this," I chirped, as I slapped down a $10-dollar bill, took our tickets, and flounced away.

We watched a couple of bands and then there

was a two-hour break for dinner. We walked through downtown Lincoln and decided on an Italian restaurant. As he held the door open for me, he whispered in my ear, "I'm paying for dinner. Don't even try to stop me."

My stomach lurched. If he held open a door for me AND paid for dinner, then this had the veneer of a date. My defenses weakened.

The next day at church, I tried to ignore him. But he was relentless, grinning at me from three pews away, walking next to me in the hallway after the service was over. He wore me down with phone calls, emails, and the ultimate invitation: he had joined a community choir working on Handel's *Messiah*, and he asked if I would like to be in the choir as well. So every Sunday at 2:30, he picked me up and drove me to a Baptist church in downtown Omaha. He would saunter off to the bass section after dropping me off to the altos, and then we would find each other two hours later and go home. Those Sunday drives to Omaha afforded the opportunity to talk about our faith, our missions, our past relationships. And I constantly reminded myself that we were just friends. Nothing beyond that going on at all.

One night he brought me flowers at work. A co-worker saw them and said, "Those are really nice! That was sweet of your boyfriend to bring them to you."

"He's not my boyfriend," I said.

"Well he's certainly auditioning for the part with those flowers," he said.

After a while, I became quite used to the idea of being with Tilney forever. He really was my Lloyd Dobler.

The night before our *Messiah* concert, I was trying to leave his sister's house. Tilney and I stood at the door. He hadn't been sleeping much, so I poked him in the chest and told him to go to bed. He took my hand in his and we stood there, looking at each other.

"Julie, sometimes I really want to kiss you," he said.

"Sometimes, I really want you to kiss me," I said.

"But then I think I shouldn't because I have a cold," he said.

"That should never be a reason to not kiss me," I said.

He put his hands on my cheeks, pulled me closer, and kissed me—the most pure, gentle, perfect kiss I had ever experienced. It was the first—and only time so far—that I felt someone was kissing me out of genuine love and care and respect, not purely driven by hormones. It was exhilarating and terrifying.

He was considerate. Like Lloyd Dobler steering Diane Court away from broken glass in the middle of the street, Tilney showed concern for my needs and was horribly sweet. If I fell asleep on the couch, he covered me with a blanket. I was often at his sister's house when he got home from work, and before he even took off his coat, he would find me and kiss me hello. By the end of November, we were exclusive. We saw each other daily, and we were as physical as our value system would allow (cuddling, kissing, holding hands). At the time, I was uncharacteristically needy. The 17 credit hours had to be successfully completed or I risked not student teaching in January. I had to work to help defray college costs. And then there was the tiny issue of my father's dance with Death.

My dad's cancer actually started in his colon, but the first scan after that tumor was removed revealed a spot on his liver. Two weeks before Christmas, before heading out on a date, Tilney and I drove to the Nebraska Medical Center to visit my dad in the ICU, post-liver surgery. We stepped into the elevator and Tilney gently took my hand and squeezed it. I looked straight ahead, but out of the corner of my eye, could see him looking at me. The elevator doors opened, and the sterile rubbing alcohol-infused odor punched me in the gut. I sucked in my breath, glanced quickly at Tilney, squeezed his hand, and headed toward my dad's room.

"Don't feel like you have to come in," I said, as we walked down the fluorescent-lit hallway.

"Why wouldn't I come in?" Tilney asked.

"I don't know—I don't know what he'll look like, what the room will smell like and I don't want you to feel like you have to. I won't stay long and then we can go see the movie," I said.

We had arrived at my dad's room, and Tilney dropped my hand.

"I'm coming in," he said. "I'm here for you." He tucked my hair behind my ear and kissed me on the cheek.

I took a deep breath, blinked back tears, and opened the door. It was never my intention to cry in front of Tilney, because crying is weakness, and I didn't want him to see me weak.

My dad, my strong dad who built a deck and could pack a moving truck with ease and let me dance on his feet, lay motionless, covered in white hospital blankets. My mom sat in the corner working on some crafting project. She stood up when she heard us come in.

"Hi!" she said, a little too cheerfully.

"Hi," I said, as I hugged her.

"How's he doing?" I asked.

"Really, pretty good. He's just in a lot of pain," she said.

And no wonder. He already had a horizontal incision across his stomach from the colon surgery. Now a vertical scar ran the length of his torso, creating a giant cross on his body. Tubes flowed out of his arms and from under the blankets, a cacophony of beeps from various monitors told those in charge whether he was living or dying. I walked closer to him, and he struggled to emerge from his drugged haze.

"Who's here?" he asked, eyes still closed.

"It's me. I mean, it's Julie. And Tilney is here too," I said.

I worried that maybe he would be embarrassed that I brought Tilney to this vulnerable place. But maybe the morphine would allow him to forget. I stood next to his bed and held his hand, but said nothing. What could I say? Tell him about my rhetoric teacher's sudden compassion when I broke down in her office the previous day? Tell him about the James Bond movie Tilney and I were going to see later that night? Everything in my life, under the microscope of cancer, was irrelevant and pointless. So I said nothing. Just stood there and held his hand.

I didn't cry in the room with my dad, and not because I worried about what Tilney would think. I didn't cry because I didn't want to disappoint my dad. Tears meant I doubted his ability to fight and survive, and I wanted to show him I knew he could live. I needed him to live.

Fifteen minutes felt like hours, and I couldn't take it anymore. I squeezed my dad's hand, hugged my mom, and we left. Tilney and I walked to the elevator, hands at our sides. I felt shell-shocked. I opened my mouth to say something, anything—cracking jokes in situations like these is my forte—but every time I opened my mouth, I couldn't speak, and tears welled in my eyes. We waited in silence at the elevator, still not touching. The massive lump in my throat nearly made me vomit. We stepped into the elevator and when the door closed I sobbed. I sobbed the breath-taking, shoulder-shaking, hopeless sobs of a daughter convinced her dad was about to die. Tilney pulled me to him and stroked my hair.

"Hey," he whispered. "He's gonna be fine. God isn't done with him on earth yet."

Tilney's words made me sob harder, and I pulled away, annoyed at the cliché he threw at me, placating words to try and stem the tears. I fished around in my purse for a tissue, found a crumpled one that, let's face it, had probably been used already, and blew my nose. I stopped the tears and stared up at the elevator lights to watch our progress down to the parking garage.

"Yeah. Thanks," I said.

We drove to the movie in silence. We drove home

from the movie in silence. When we arrived at my house, I started to get out of the car, and he grabbed my hand.

"Hey, you know if you need anything, I'm here, right?" he said.

"Yeah. I know," I said.

We never talked about my elevator breakdown again.

Tilney spent another month completing all sorts of Lloyd Dobler-esque tasks. Surprise me at work? Check. Email me every day? Check. Randomly tell me how beautiful I am? Check. Play piano duets with me? Check. Play the piano while I sing, then tell me how gorgeous my voice is? Check. Leave little notes on my car? Check. Craft a cute little saying (puss och kram—hug and a kiss in Swedish) to take the place of "I love you" at the end of emails and notes? Check. Despite all my journal entries that appealed to the logical side of my brain that knew I was headed for a major heartbreak, I fell for him completely. I was tired of fighting his acts of kindness, and frankly, I was tired of my independence. Though we never spoke of that elevator breakdown again, it was actually a relief to collapse in his arms when I was at my weakest and not have to pretend I was strong. I wanted to have that safety net forever.

By the time Christmas rolled around, we were straight-up disgusting. Kissing whenever possible—including at red lights— holding hands every time we walked side by side, staring at each other like we were auditioning for the *Twilight* movie, over a decade before its release. At the church Christmas party, my brother was Santa

Claus. Tilney, to be silly, sat on his lap. Not missing a beat, my brother asked, "Young man, what do you want for Christmas?"

Tilney looked at me—I was in his eye line but out of earshot—and (my brother told me later) said, "I can't tell you because you're related to her."

On Christmas day, we saw *Toy Story 2* with his family, who came to town for the holiday. Then we headed to my house to exchange gifts. I handed him mine first.

"This is a book that I first saw at BYU, and ever since, I wanted to give it to someone I really love," I said.

He opened the wrapping to see *I Like You* by Sandol Stoddard Warburg.

"Will you read it to me?" he asked.

I sat up straight on the couch, cleared my throat, and Tilney snuggled next to me, his head on my shoulder so he could follow along as I read the whole book to him. I didn't use voices, I wasn't silly or childish. This was me, using an author's words to tell Tilney just how much I loved him. When I reached the last page, Tilney turned his head into my shoulder and kissed my arm.

I bent my head down and kissed the top of his head, then stroked the side of his face. He looked up at me, so serious, and said "Thank you for reading that to me. I like you too."

I smiled, and he softly kissed my lips, then rested his head on my shoulder again. In that moment, I was sure of only one thing: I was sitting on the couch with my husband. Amidst the uncertainty of my dad's health, my student teaching, and Tilney's move to Utah, marrying him was the only thing I was absolutely certain about.

After several minutes he said, "Okay, now it's time for your gift. You have to open it in stages."

He handed me a stack of wrapped presents.

"Where do I start?" I asked.

He fished out a small, flat, square package from the stack.

"Start here."

I slowly peeled the tape from the wrapping paper, and found pocket hand warmers.

"Those are to keep your hands warm while I'm gone, since I won't be here to hold them for you," he said.

I laughed. "Nice call."

He handed me a wrapped rectangular box next. It was quite light, and I had no clue what it could possibly be. I shook it lightly, and heard something like paper swishing inside. I unwrapped it—a box of peach herbal tea.

"This is for you to drink at night when it's really cold and we can't snuggle on the couch," he said.

I leaned over and kissed him quickly. "Thank you. This is really sweet."

"Okay, last one," he said, as he patted a rather large gift.

Not caring to save the paper, I ripped into it, and before me was a set of green flannel sheets, decorated with moose and pine trees.

"Uh, no one—not even my mom—has ever given me sheets as a gift before," I said.

"Well, I saw these, and I thought about how you are

always cold. And I thought if you had flannel sheets, then you'd be warmer at night. And I thought this pattern was perfect for you—for us—because the moose and pine trees remind me of Sweden, and Sweden reminds you of me. So now, whenever you fall asleep, you're guaranteed to think of me as the last thing before you dream," he said.

Most people would look at these gifts—hand warmers, herbal tea, and sheets for heck's sake—and be insulted or confused or angry. But his explanations of each gift screamed at me "I'm leaving Nebraska, but I'm not leaving you."

We actually had talked about getting married a couple of times during our brief courtship, and before we knew what hit us, December was nearly over, which meant he had to go to BYU to return to his studies, and I had to get ready to student teach. One night at a grocery store before he left, he told me he wasn't planning on dating other girls there.

"Oh, you should," I said.

"I should? Why?"

"Because you'll only realize none of them are as perfect for you as I am," I replied.

I was that confident that we would marry; the thought of him dating other girls didn't bother me. In my mind, he could try to date other girls, but he'd just be thinking about me all night anyway. I had never been so secure in a relationship, and I have never been so cavalier since.

The day he left, I stopped to say goodbye before I

went to work. We held each other in the hallway of his sister's home and tried to make small talk.

"It's ridiculous to try a conversation," he said.

I laughed.

He touched my cheek and his face grew serious. "So just kiss me," he said.

He felt so soft, so warm, so strong. And I felt safe.

When he left, I was under the impression that we were still a couple—and for about a month, despite the distance, I still felt like his girlfriend. We emailed, talked on the phone, discussed where I could live when I moved to Utah. I planned to move to Utah four months after he did, partially because so many of my friends lived there and partially because he was there. Between his busy school schedule, my student teaching, and my dad's chemo treatments, the phone calls disappeared and the emails became less frequent. But in the weeks leading up to my move, he called with greater frequency. Two weeks before my move, he called me after church.

"Hey, when will you be here, again?"

"Memorial Day. I should get there on Memorial Day," I said.

"Okay, good. I want to help you move in," he said.

"You don't have to do that," I said.

"I know I don't have to. I want to."

I pulled into Orem, Utah on Memorial Day and called Tilney. No answer. I waited for about 30 minutes and called him again. Still no answer. After an hour, I started unloading my car, trying him two more times. He never answered his phone.

He waited two weeks to call me back.

"Hey, sorry about the move," he said.

"That's okay—I was able to take care of it. What's up?"

"I was wondering if you'd like to come over for dinner," he said.

"Sure. That would be great. When?"

"Let's see . . . I'm pretty busy . . . how does two weeks from tonight sound?" he asked.

Two weeks? I thought. I'll have been in Utah for a month by then, a month of not seeing him. What was happening?

"Oh," I said, "Um, sure. Two weeks from tonight?"

"Yeah, that will work. I'll pencil you in," he said.

Those two weeks gave me adequate time to assess our relationship and its future. I made multiple pro and con lists. Pro: kind, funny, musical, smart, hot. Con: been pulling away for a while, maybe too Mormony, too optimistic. I pondered what I could do if I didn't stay in Utah—after all, he was the primary reason I moved. Maybe I could still get into that master's program I'd wanted to do in Omaha. By the time the dinner date rolled around, I was determined to break up with him before he could break up with me. I couldn't completely ignore how sure I was that I would marry him, but as I thought about how distant he'd become between February and May, I worried that something similar could happen if we did marry. What if I couldn't lose any baby weight? What if I wanted to work? What if I didn't want to move wherever his future job might take us? If he didn't want to make our relationship work with a four-month separation, could I really trust him for the rest of my life? So I decided I would not only start the conversation, but I would end the relationship.

I arrived at his apartment and we stumbled through awkward conversation about nothing that mattered, and clearly about nothing memorable. After he cleared away the spaghetti and meatballs, I said, "So I don't want to see you anymore. At all. In any capacity."

His eyes widened.

"Not even as friends?" he asked.

"We can't go back to that. It's clear you don't want to be with me, and 'friends' doesn't work for me. I have enough 'friends.' I don't need more," I said.

He lowered his head. Was he crying? I tried to look at his face, angling my face upward. Nope. He wasn't crying. I sat back in my chair.

"I guess I wanted a clear sign from God that I should marry you," he started, "and I never got it."

"What kind of sign were you looking for?" I asked.

"You know, the voice of God telling me you were The One, or a really nice warm feeling that you're a good choice for a spouse. It hasn't happened, and I don't think it will," he said.

"Well, then I guess that settles it," I said.

I grabbed my purse off his couch, opened the door and headed to my car. He followed me out.

He called after me, "I feel like I should start singing 'Each Life That Touches Ours For Good.'"

I turned around and rolled my eyes at him. That's

a hymn sung at funerals. Who references hymns in the middle of a breakup?

A month passed, and I still got updates about how he was doing from his sister. He wanted to meet, and initially, I had flashes of hope. He wanted me back! Why else would he call?

To justify his actions, that's why.

"You know, Julie," he began, as we walked along an access road behind the condo I was renting, "You read way too much into our relationship."

"I'm sorry?" I couldn't believe what I was hearing.

"You thought there was more to us than there actually was."

"How so?" I asked, daring him to tell me how I misinterpreted the months we spent dating.

"You forced me into a relationship. I didn't want a relationship with you. I cannot be the clichéd missionary that comes home and marries the first girl he dates," he said.

"So this is about pride?" I asked.

"Not exactly," he said.

"Then what?"

He didn't have much of an explanation, but he finally said, "I don't know how you thought we were serious, other than the fact that I gave you roses before I left. I regret that. I shouldn't have given you roses. I shouldn't have ever given you flowers if I knew you would think it meant I loved you. I didn't."

Had he completely forgotten my elevator breakdown? The nights reading books on the couch?

The foot rubs? The flowers at work? The night he and I played cards with Lauren and her husband, and at the end of the night he said, "I'm sorry if I was staring at you tonight—you're just so beautiful"?

Had he completely forgotten Christmas?

Sure, it had been eight months earlier, but really—had he forgotten?

By the time we returned from the walk, I'd heard enough. Still in the middle of rationalizing his choice to break up with me, I climbed the stairs to my condo.

"Can't I see you smile one more time?" he called from the bottom of the stairs.

"No," I said, and I slammed my front door.

When we first dated, he was the closest thing to Lloyd Dobler I've ever known. Completely attentive, sickeningly sweet, Tilney was the first guy I unequivocally believed I would marry.

His wife's name is Abby.

# The Part Where Jane Austen Rolls Over In Her Grave

Confession: I have tried online dating.

It feels so shameful, so dirty, so pathetic. With the exception of one year on Match.com, I have stuck to LDS dating sites in an effort to meet nice men who share my values. I've learned that apparently my values include being treated like garbage. Case in point: when I was 28, a 72 year-old Italian sent me a message, wanting to get to know me. I wrote back, "I'm sorry, but we have too much of an age difference for me to feel comfortable." His response: "Don't you want children? You are running out of time, while I can have children as long as I want. You can't afford to be so picky."

Classy.

At first glance, I think Jane Austen would have loved online dating. All those letters her characters wrote-- what is a message through a dating site if not a letter? But Austen's dedication to the power of letters skewed my expectations of online correspondence. Rare is the man who writes a multi-paragraph expounding of my virtues. Common is the man who writes "hey sexy" and "what you up to" void of English writing mechanics and personality. Austen also valued chastity within fledgling relationships--and the distance between me and the few online suitors I've experienced certainly fostered chastity. What would have ruffled Austen's feathers is the illusion of online dating. It is really quite easy to put forth one persona online yet be completely different in person. Here are some of my favorites.

Randy: a divorced father of one living in a nearby state. His profile stated he was looking for a serious relationship. We started slowly, with emails through the website. We moved to online chatting, then to personal emails, and graduated to phone calls. We could talk for hours. We met in person, went on one date, and it was weeks before I heard from him again. When pressed about his silence he said, "I'm not ready to date." THEN WHY ARE YOU ON A DATING SITE, YOU FREAK?

Hank: a single eternal student living in a nearby state. He and I moved quickly out of the site's email client and into online chatting, phone calls, and personal emails. This went off and on for two years. We met in person. I met his parents. They loved me. After meeting his parents, I waited for an email, a phone call, a chat online, semaphore flags or smoke signals. Too proud to contact him myself, I didn't hear from him for four months. When he happened to drive through Omaha and called to see if I wanted to meet for lunch, I said yes, so I could ask him in person where he had been for four months. His response?

"I don't do long distance relationships all that well."

"You couldn't have sent me one email explaining that?"

"No. Why? Did you take it personally?"

"How else should I have taken it?"

He had no response for that question, but offered this gem:

"I like being with you when I can, but I can't be exclusive with you. So, can I still call you?"

"No. No you may not still call me. I am not your back-up plan for whenever you feel like it."

At this point, he took out his cell phone and said, "So do you want me to delete your number out of my cell phone?" He flipped the phone open and started scrolling through numbers.

"Yes. Yes, please delete my number, you jackass."

"Okay." He pushed a button or two. "Done."

I didn't want to be the one watching him walk away, so I rolled my eyes at him, got up and walked out of the restaurant. WHY DID YOU TALK TO ME FOR TWO YEARS, YOU FREAK?

Barry: a single, successful computer programmer who lived two states away. We also moved quickly out of the website and into personal email, chat, and phone calls. For four months we had near-daily contact. We made plans to meet. On the appointed day, he could not be found. I had traveled many miles (to see other friends, too, but still . . .).

He stood me up.

He called three days later when I was in Las Vegas with a friend. He said something came up at work. THEN WHY DIDN'T YOU CALL ME THAT DAY, YOU FREAK?

Kendall: a single, successful engineer who lived in a neighboring state. We kinda sorta went on a couple of maybe kinda dates. We spent many hours on the phone in which I learned that he liked gardening, weather, and Mitt Romney. He once let me stay at his house as I drove to grad school in Ohio. Two years later on my way back to Nebraska after graduation, he invited me over for dinner. "Let me give you the tour of my house," he said.

"Um, I've had the tour. I stayed here two years ago," I said.

"You did? No. No way. Really?"

"Yep, I sure did. I even showered here."

"Oh. I forgot."

THEN WHY ARE YOU EVEN STILL TALKING TO ME, YOU FREAK?

I want my Captain Wentworth, or even a Mr. Darcy, but apparently the online dating world is chock-full of Wickhams. I know online dating works for some people; I have several friends who met their spouses that way. However, I seem to attract the true cretins of the establishment. And I'm pretty sure I'm done with that racket. Online dating is just one more place to be completely rejected, and I tend to get enough of that in 3-D land. But as I've toiled in the bleak landscape of online dating, I've noticed some common themes with all guys.

1. Every single guy loves the outdoors. Every single one of them. What makes this so difficult for me to comprehend is that when I meet someone in 3-D Land, his affinity for nature is rarely first-date conversation material. So why do so many men online feel it necessary to tell me that they love skiing, SCUBA diving, camping, hiking, mountain biking, tree hugging, squirrel hunting,

and living in yurts? Don't any of these guys watch sports? Which leads me to . . .

2. None of these guys watch sports. I can't figure out if this is their way of trying to pull a bait-and-switch on unsuspecting women. But if I read one more profile that says, "Don't really watch sports, but I play all of them: golf, tennis, football, basketball, ultimate Frisbee, squash and cricket," I am going to call shenanigans on him and make him fess up that he calls in sick to work every third Thursday and Friday in March--the first round of the NCAA men's basketball tournament. Watching sports is actually rather important to me. Best dating advice I got from a co-worker, after we spent 45 minutes dissecting the problems with the now-defunct Bowl Championship Series: "Jules, hearing you talk like that is sexy as hell. You need to stop dating guys who don't watch sports." I would. If I could find one who will admit that he does.

3. As far as I can tell, men online seek out women who are 12 or more years younger than they are. This means that men my age as of this writing are looking at women who are 28, and the only men looking at me are 50 and older. I don't know how the 28 year-old women feel about this, but every time I see that another man in his late 50s has looked at my profile, I want to vomit. In one week, five men over 55 looked at my profile. None of them look like George Clooney. They all look like Jim Varney. If they did look like Clooney, maybe I'd be more open to pursuing something.

4. All online dating eventually suffers from what I call The Gatsby Effect. If you slept through junior English (as

most of my students do), you may not remember the relationship between Jay Gatsby and Daisy Buchanan. Jay and Daisy were lovers, against Daisy's parents' wishes. So they married her off to a complete dirtbag named Tom when Jay went off to war. But Gatsby loved him some Daisy. What I teach my students every year is that Gatsby loved the idea of Daisy, not actually Daisy herself. When he does reconnect with her years later, he loves Daisy of 1917, not Daisy of 1922. He won't let go of that 1917 illusion. This is online dating.

People can be downright charming and witty when they have all day to craft an email. Meet in person, and the conversation can be downright painful. And it's really easy to fall for the illusion that they are quick-witted and charming. Additionally, many guys I've met online use photos that are at least five or six years old. I think I've established that I'm hardly a specimen of ideal femininity, but at least my photos are current. Guys shouldn't be too surprised when they see me, but I have surely been surprised when I see them. Physical attraction can only get me so far, though. If he can't carry a conversation, there's no point in going much further. And most of the time in person, the guys turn out to be about as exciting as Eeyore.

5. When it comes right down to it, plain and simple, it's a minefield of desperation. I include myself in that. I wouldn't check the sites obsessively if I wasn't feeling the horrifying pressure of wanting to marry before my dad dies. Which, when he was diagnosed with cancer, became even more real. But it seems like the

desperation includes a hell of a lot of pickiness, too. Apparently beggars can be choosers when five times as many women are looking for a spouse.

But I'm ready to close for good the online dating chapter of my life. And I have Christian doctrine to support me on this choice. In his epistle to the Philippians, Paul advised, "...whatever is true, whatever is worthy of respect, whatever is just, whatever is pure, whatever is lovely, whatever is commendable, if something is excellent or praiseworthy, think about these things" (Philippians 4:8).

Most men in the online world have not been worthy of my respect. Nothing lovely has resulted in my online dating experience, nothing commendable and certainly nothing praiseworthy.

So why am I seeking after these things?

In *You've Got Mail*, Greg Kinnear warns Meg Ryan that the computer she is so often glued to is not her friend. It's obvious irony—as the viewer, we know the man she is talking to via computer is her professional nemesis. Definitely not a friend. One of the easiest things to do when your relationships are mediated by a computer is lie, lie, lie. Whether it's posting photos from five years ago or using a thesaurus to mask a limited vocabulary, or taking two days to return an email so it can endure several edits from multiple friends, much of online dating is grounded in deception.

And in my experience with online dating, the easiest lie to tell is "I'm divorced."

Willoughby and I were friends in high school. He was a rare breed of masculinity—the epitome of tall, dark, and handsome, a total jock but sensitive enough to be in choir AND show choir. He was far out of my league, but he was also a huge flirt, and I never rebuffed any of his fake advances. He went to a military academy for college and during his first year there, he joined the LDS church. This was incredibly exciting. He was the second friend of mine from high school to join the church. And while I am truly, truly grateful for this decision they made for their own salvation, I will admit I was also pretty stoked that there were two more marriageable guys in the fold. Willoughby served a mission in Texas and we wrote the whole two years he was gone. When he returned to college I drove to see him. When I went on my mission, he wrote me a couple of letters, and when I had been on my mission for six months, his wedding announcement arrived. I was happy for him—we were always just friends—and he was marrying a girl well within his league in the St. Louis Temple.

Four years later I was living in Salt Lake City and had just moved in with the best roommates in the world. On a snowy January Saturday, I set up my computer and checked my email. I squinted at the screen, not believing what I was seeing: an email from Willoughby. I checked the subject line. It didn't look like spam, so I opened the email. He muddled through some small talk, and then confessed that his wife was making choices that made marriage to her impossible. He was going to get a divorce. He wanted someone to talk to.

His family, like Wickham's, did not understand his decision to join the LDS church, and he was concerned about their reaction to the end of his marriage. I still don't know why he thought I would be a good sounding board. I tend to underestimate my impact on people, and Willoughby was a perfect example of that. I'm sure he had plenty of other LDS friends he could have turned to. But he turned to me. I was still smarting from losing Knightley and Tilney, so I was able to approach the situation with Willoughby as strictly a friendly endeavor.

At first.

The emails were slow in those first months—maybe once every two weeks, sometimes once a month. By the spring, the emails were every other day, and we chatted online a couple times a week as well. He moved for his job, and his wife was not going with him. He never told me the exact reasoning behind their split, but he was devastated, and I suppose he needed a friend. So I became that friend. Except that by May, I was liking him more than just a friend should. Online chats lasted two or more hours, and we would talk about books, movies, cars, relationships, and our faith. It was the conversations about our faith that reminded me I really shouldn't fall for him, as he was still legally married.

<Willoughby: Sigh...stressful day. What would you do if you had to meet with a divorce attorney?>

<Julie: I'm so sorry. I don't know. I'd definitely pray— not only for you but also for both attorneys, that they won't let things spin out of control in anger.>

<Julie: Sorry, that seems like such a copout answer.>

<Willoughby: No! It makes sense. That's really good advice. Thank you. I'm so blessed to have you in my life right now. I wouldn't want to be doing this alone.>

The rest of the summer was bliss, or at least as much bliss as a computer could allow. In early July, we were chatting online when he typed in, "Do you want to video conference?"

All of my high school insecurities resurfaced. I'm not pretty enough. I'm too fat. He will see me on his screen and find a creative way to disconnect and never talk to me again. I'm not a stupid girl, and eight months of dating Knightley had made me pretty tech-savvy. But eight months of dating Knightley had also taught me that sometimes I can pretend to be stupid. I feigned girlish incompetence and typed, "I don't know how to set it up."

"That's okay. My hair looks awful," he typed back.

I laughed, took a deep breath and typed, "I'll figure it out."

And ten minutes later, I was looking at Willoughby.

He was just as good looking as ever—perhaps even more so. The boyish cuteness I remembered from high school had evolved into a manly handsomeness. "Hot" lacked the depth now etched in his face; he was dashing. Breathtaking. Still so far out of my league. After high school, missions, and college, I still placed him on a pedestal that no ladder I owned could possibly reach. And this is where I have a really tough time figuring out why people come into my life.

Sometimes, people come into my life out of obvious

connections. I think of the people I work with who are some of my dearest friends—I don't think there's always a grand plan that brings together those particular people at any particular time. We happen to have each made choices that led us to that spot, and we capitalize on that opportunity.

But with dating, I often look for divine intervention. Perhaps because I always thought it would take a miracle of biblical proportions to get me married. Maybe because church youth leaders told me twisted stories about couples who "just knew" they were meant for each other after two dates. Disney and other sanitized versions of fairy tales have nothing on Mormons. If God does everything for a reason—a dogma not particular to Mormons, I might add—then that includes placing people in my life at certain times. There was a reason Wickham visited me before I left for my mission, there was a reason Knightley came into my life days after Wickham destroyed my heart; I could craft reasons for meeting just about any man ever. And Willoughby was no exception. His presence in my life was divinely inspired. What other explanation could there be? Coincidence? Pshaw.

Yes, I was supporting him emotionally as he worked through the end of his marriage. But he made me want to be a better person. Our conversations made it clear that he was a much better Christian than I was, and I wanted to rise to his level. He prayed often. He read his scriptures daily. He asked what I thought of certain verses, and we talked openly about how life and faith often seemed incompatible. But knowing Willoughby compelled me to pray more, to study scripture, to evaluate what role I wanted my faith to play in day-to-day life. I hoped that reconnecting with him in such a deep way at this point in our lives was the miracle of biblical proportions I'd been waiting for.

A week after our video conference I was in Omaha, telling my brother goodbye for two years as he went to Brazil for his mission. Willoughby was on an exercise in the woods—an unplanned military exercise—so I didn't hear from him for a week. When he returned, he emailed me an apology: "I'm sorry it took so long to get to you, and I'm sorry I wasn't available when Brent left. Let me know what I can do for you." And so it continued for another month. Emails, long chats online—we talked nearly every day through the rest of the summer.

And then.

I'm not sure exactly how it happened, and even my journal is a little sketchy documenting how he pulled away. But he did. First, 9/11 happened. Four days later was the car accident and I wasn't as available (or coherent) as I had been. A week after my car accident, his divorce was finalized, which made me think that perhaps our relationship would start to morph into something a little more serious. Instead, he slowly disappeared. And within the span of his slow disappearance, Knightley got married, then Wickham, then Tilney. Christmas came and went with no word from Willoughby, and I wondered if he had been deployed to Afghanistan. I emailed him every so often to check in, but the responses were short and at times cryptic. So I quit emailing.

And then in February, he sent an email, dropping the name "Anna" as if I was supposed to know who that was. Turns out, she was his fiancée, and they'd be getting married soon. I wrote back a quick congratulations, removed him from my chat list and email contacts, laid on my bed, and cried.

I've often thought about Willoughby and what I was supposed to learn from that experience. True, we were friends before he was married, so perhaps my hope that we would end up together was immature and uncalled for. But I thought that he might be my Wentworth. After years of both of us being with people who weren't right, we would find each other and finally be happy in a way we couldn't have been at any other time in our lives.

Instead, I ended up feeling like Duckie one more time. I wasn't sure how many more times I'd survive that kind of disappointment.

Three years after my first engagement fell
through.

# Divorce Crisis Hotline Take 2

Every so often I would place an offering on the altar of "please-don't-let-me-die-alone." If I think it will take a miracle of biblical proportions to get me married, then I ought to show what I am willing to sacrifice in order for that miracle to happen. Namely, sacrifice my pride.

Over and over and over again.

More often than I should, the offering means that I swallow my pride, log on to a stupid dating site and send a message to the least offensive person who relatively matches my criteria. So one spring day, two weeks before a paid subscription was going to run out on an LDS dating site, I did so. I sent a brief message to Col. Brandon (Hi! How are you? What do you teach? Bye!), who looked interesting. This is usually a safe offering to lay down, as guys never respond to me online, much like they never respond to me in real life.

Digression: I am apparently repulsive to men within my demographic. Figuring out why has been rather difficult, because my married male friends and my girl friends tell me they are mystified by my single status. Men way outside my key demographic express interest in me though. The problem is that those men are either 20 years older than me or 20 years younger than me. I'm not okay with either of those extremes. Therefore, sending a message to a man within 4-6 years of my own age was a completely safe offering. He wouldn't message me back, and I could go on cursing God for allowing me to exist as a single woman.

Seriously, strike me dead, already.

Except the relatively interesting man did send me a message back. A long message. A sweet message. And at the end of that message, he was honest:

"I have been under divorce proceedings for over a year now but expect it to be complete in the next few weeks. I just don't want there to be any deception about this. Hope this is ok, as I just signed up for this site a couple of days ago."

I appreciated his honesty, but I did pause. It had been 10 years since Willoughby's divorce, and I certainly did not want to repeat being the confidante, being Duckie to someone who would eventually just leave me and marry someone else. This was different, though. I didn't know this guy prior. He had no expectation of friendship. He was on a dating site for crying out loud. What did he expect to happen? So I wrote him back.

I referenced the situation with Willoughby, and that I had kind of helped him through a rough time, and told the guy that he could write when he wanted, if he wanted. I told him I was sorry for his divorce, but I appreciated his honesty. I clicked send, and didn't think I would hear from him for a while, which for me meant it would be at least a week before he wrote again.

By his standards, though, "a while" meant "less than 12 hours" because that's when the next email came. I was confused. What did he think he was doing? He was still married, on a dating site, and I gave him the perfect out to never write me again. Why was he writing? He wasn't supposed to be writing. This is not the way my life works out, I thought. He is being too nice, too attentive, in too short a period of time. And with every email I sent, knowing eventually he would stop writing, he lobbed a sweeter email back at me. It was confusing and irritating. And I loved every minute of it.

Within two weeks, I was hooked. I relayed some of the information to a friend at school, trying not to dissolve into a puddle of absolute mush.

"Oh my gosh, I've never seen you like this. You're completely smitten," he said.

I blushed, tried to hide my smile, but protesting was useless. I was completely smitten. At the end of those two weeks, I was hopeful that the divorce was finalized and that we would meet soon.

After two weeks, the divorce wasn't finalized.

I struggled with that fact all summer, as we both tried to figure out what kind of relationship we wanted from each other. I was adamant that we be very careful and keep our emails, texts, and phone conversations on a strictly 'friend' basis. But he seemed to be dissatisfied with that course of action. Flirt after flirt after flirt. Photo after photo after photo. Pictures of him cooking, pictures of his kids. Why send me pictures of your kids? I thought to myself after the first time he sent me a picture of them. It made no sense. If we were just friends, why would he want me to know anything about his kids?

Throughout the course of our relationship, there was only one day in which we did not talk, text, or email. And that one day was when he took his kids camping and had no Internet access. And to make up for it, he emailed me twice on the day he got home. After three weeks of emails and hundreds of texts, we graduated to phone calls. Nearly every night between 9 and 11 p.m., he would call. Ever the gentleman, he wanted to call me, wanted to court me. He would text me one word: "Talk?" And I would text back "Yes!" And he would call. Some nights we would talk only for a few minutes. Most nights, though, we talked for well over an hour, sometimes two or three.

It had been so long since a man had wanted to talk to me that it took a while for me to relearn how that worked. I was reserved at first--and I was hyper-aware that legally he was still married. There were things I wanted to tell him but couldn't, because he couldn't completely be mine. Talking to him was simultaneously the high point and the low point of my day.

My birthday approached, and I hoped he would surprise me with a visit or flowers. The night before, I told him I'd be at my parents' for my birthday dinner.

"Oh? Your birthday is tomorrow?" he said.

"Are you sassing me?" I asked.

"No . . . I knew your birthday was coming up, but I didn't realize it was this weekend," he said.

"Oh," I said, trying to not sound too deflated. It wasn't like him to forget a detail like my birthday, but we weren't officially a couple, so I didn't really have a right to be upset.

After my birthday dinner, it was time for presents, but first, my mom handed me the phone. I figured one of the gifts was from my sister Deanne, and I was to call her so she could listen to me open what she gave me. Instead, my mom said, "Scroll through the caller ID."

I looked at her, quizzically, and she had a hidden smile on her face.

"Dad called you?" I said.

"Keep scrolling."

"Jennie called you?" I said.

"Scroll one more."

The third name I saw?

His.

While I was preoccupied with the phone, my dad had gone back to his office and retrieved a white box. He was standing behind me when I saw the number, and he placed the box in front of me. The return address was his hometown.

I almost threw up.

The story goes like this:

He called my mom to get my address, but she hesitated a bit. I had barely told her about him, not wanting to get her hopes up, and now he was asking for my address. He told my mom he didn't want to ask me for my address, because he wanted to surprise me and didn't want me to know a gift was on its way.

He could sense her hesitation, so he said, "If you'd feel more comfortable, give me your address and I can send it to you."

She gave him their address and he mailed a present for me to my mom and dad's house. Then he called that morning to make sure it arrived.

My hands shook as I opened the mailing box. Inside, I found a long, thin box—the kind of box that jewelry comes in. My heart raced. I had heard rumors that jewelry was a sure-fire way for a man to express his feelings for a woman. I ran my fingers over the box, and for a split-second considered what might be inside. Too long and narrow for a ring, but not quite wide enough for a necklace. I pulled off the lid to find a perfect bracelet of gold ovals connected by small silver links. I don't wear bracelets, but this one was thin and delicate and didn't bother me like a watch or other bracelets do. I was completely swooning. After I left my parents, I called him.

"You, sir, are amazing," I said.

"Happy birthday. I wish I could be there to make you dinner and a cake, and just sit on the porch with you and watch the sunset. I knew that wasn't going to be possible, so I wanted to give you something special," he said.

We chatted a few minutes more and then he let me go.

Four hours later, as the clock turned from not-my-birthday to my actual-birthday, he texted me.

"I wanted to be the very first to wish you Happy birthday on your actual birthday. Hope I didn't wake you, but if I did, I hope you fall back asleep with a smile on your face."

All those who believe we were "just friends," please signify by raising your right hand.

Those opposed by the same sign.

Three days after my birthday, he called in the middle of the day. That was unusual, so I answered the phone, worried.

"Hey, are you okay?" I said.

"Yes! I am fine, and I am wonderful. I am so happy. I just had to call and tell you how happy I am," he said.

"Oh! Good! I'm so glad you're happy!"

"I don't think you understand. I'm so happy, and so ready to move forward with my life, and I want you to be happy, too."

"I am happy," I said.

"No, I mean, I want you to be so, so happy, and I want us to move forward," he said. "You're so amazing. You are precious. You are so perfect, and I am just so happy you are in my life."

Tears sprang to my eyes.

"You're so sweet," I said.

"Okay, I have to go, but I just wanted to tell you how happy I am, and I will talk to you later tonight, okay?"

"Sounds good. Drive safely," I said.

And we did talk that night.

And the next night. And two nights later, as I readied myself for a choir concert, we chatted. I had sent him YouTube links to my favorite songs the choir had learned that summer. "Give Me Jesus" I loved for the harmonies and the build-up to the end. "McKay" was a song I hated at first, but eventually grew to love. And then the piece de resistance: "Amor de Mi Alma." Its composer, Z. Randall Stroope was my former choir director at the University of Nebraska-Omaha, and while I didn't care for his personality, the man can write music. He writes absolutely soul-stirring music that I feel in every ligament of my body. His harmonies make me weep; it is impossible to sing a Stroope choral arrangement and not be moved. "Amor de Mi Alma" was no different, and I'll be honest, all summer as we rehearsed that song, I often thought of Col. Brandon. The text of the song is incredibly romantic, but I didn't send Col. Brandon the YouTube video of that song because of the lyrics; I sent it to him because it was one example of the kind of music we sang.

"Did you like the songs?" I asked.

"I really did," he said. "I had no idea you were that talented. I mean, I guessed you were, but wow. Those songs are beautiful," he said.

"Thanks! And I'm not singing them alone, you know. I'm with a whole choir. I'm just one voice."

"I know, but the fact that you're able to learn them proves how talented you are. I'm amazed. You amaze me," he said.

"You're too sweet."

"My favorite is 'Amor de Mi Alma.' Do you know what the lyrics mean?" he said.

"Kind of. We have an English translation on the music, but we're singing it in Spanish," I said.

"It's really quite lovely," he said.

"I know."

We sat in silence for several minutes. This happened

often, and one time we talked about what our long silences really meant. For me, it meant I was trying to find a way to tell him how I really, truly felt while respecting the fact that he was still married. I never did figure out how to do that. For him, it meant he was purposely keeping himself from saying too much too soon. We often talked about how we both wanted to say what was really in our hearts, but couldn't, and this pre-concert conversation was one of those times that I felt it more deeply. I knew I cared about him before, but on this evening, I knew for sure I was falling in love with him.

That realization should have been the blazing-red neon sign warning me that it was all going to fall apart—and soon—but I was convinced this time was different. It had to be. If I was going to acknowledge the hand of God in all my prior relationships, then I had to in this one. And here is what I acknowledged. Prior to meeting Col. Brandon:

I was really building my career into something solid.

I took on the added responsibility of newspaper advising.

I was finally okay with being alone. And relatively happy about it.

After a couple of months of no action on the online dating site, I was ready to ditch it for good.

And then I met Col. Brandon, and even though his divorce wasn't final, he often told me how much he and his wife had grown apart. She'd been dating someone for almost a year, they differed greatly when it came to religion, and while he acknowledged that she was a good mother, he knew the relationship was over. I told him once that I couldn't make brownies from a box (I can make all kinds of other deliciousness, so I'm okay with that) and he said it made him happy to know that, because the only baked goods his wife ever made were brownies. He loathed them, he said. Never wanted another brownie in his life, he said. Mail me some cookies or biscotti, he said.

The day after the concert, I bought ingredients to make biscotti.

He was mostly unavailable that day, and I chalked it up to him getting ready to take his kids on vacation. We texted intermittently, but it was clear to me that something wasn't right. I awoke the next day and could feel in my bones that I was about to get hit. I tried distracting myself by working in my classroom since school was days away from starting, but every so often I cried. I had no reason to—I hadn't talked to him yet that day, and I hadn't been so sure of a relationship since Tilney. I reassured myself of his feelings for me by rereading emails and text messages, recalling my birthday dinner at my parents, reliving the phone call just three days earlier when he told me how happy he was. The tears confused me, but at the same time, I realized my soul knew something the rest of me did not. Twelve hours later, the initial strains of A Fine Frenzy's "What I Wouldn't Do" invaded my ears. It was his ringer. The perfect song to describe how I felt about him.

"Hey you," I said.

"Hi. We need to talk. And this isn't going to be easy,"

he said.

The tears I had been crying all day returned. The insecurities I've battled my entire life returned. And I listened to him explain why he couldn't talk to me anymore. As much as I felt God had brought us together (a sentiment he had shared with me as well), he was starting to feel that God was prompting him to try and repair his marriage. I was floored. I would have been less surprised if he had told me he ran a credit check on me, or that he had found recent photos of me that weren't taken in good lighting at advantageous angles. I almost think it would have hurt less if he had said I wasn't pretty enough or skinny enough to fit in his life, because those were flaws I knew existed, and girls who aren't pretty or skinny don't get to marry the man of their dreams. But to hear him say he wanted to try and repair his marriage? This made no sense to me.

I never really fell asleep that night. I closed my eyes, and cliché as it sounds, I wanted it to all be a dream, to be imagined. How could he flip on me so soon? I was devastated, and it had been a decade since I really had to manage losing someone I cared so much about. Sure, I'd had disappointments before, but this one felt so real, so permanent. I actually had let myself imagine being with him at Thanksgiving. He told me he was going to make me decorate my apartment for Christmas. I wasn't living day-to-day with him, I was building a future. To lose that future was heartwrenching.

In the months following our breakup, I medicated with work. I took on several additional jobs to keep me out of the house. I stayed at school when I didn't need to, because as soon as I walked in my door, I fell apart. Every day, I trudged from my car to the mailbox, and my heart fluttered ever-so-slightly with the possibility that "today is the day I receive a letter from him." Every day, I turned my mailbox key slowly, and opened a metal box filled with magazines, bills, and junk mail. Never a letter from Texas. But this didn't devastate me. I walked up the stairs and snuck peeks at my door, hoping for a UPS or FedEx sticker, or a note from my landlord saying there were flowers in the main office for me. When I finally faced my door, my shoulders sagged a little, and I sighed, and I resigned myself to another long day of not talking to him.

But I repeat the process the next day, and the next, and even years later as I write this, I wonder if I will ever get my mail without hoping there's a letter from him.

# Shifting Blame

About four months after Col. Brandon and I broke up, I had a terrifying dream. I was in my living room; a man was in the room with me, and he was angry. He pulled out a pistol, loaded one bullet, and shoved me onto the couch. Then he pulled the trigger. Aimed at my leg. Click. Aimed at my arm. Click. Aimed at my chest. Click. Aimed at my shoulder. Click. Aimed at my other shoulder. Click.

Aimed at my head.

Bang.

The bullet hit me square between the eyes, but I lived. I asked my lunch crew for possible interpretations. Most of the online dream dictionaries say if you dream you are shot, then it means you're feeling victimized in a situation. But my friend Marya, who is well-versed in alternative spirituality, had a more compelling explanation. Apparently, the chakra that connects the person with a higher power is right between the eyes. Her interpretation was that I am experiencing conflict within myself and my higher power.

I chewed on this for a while, and realized one of my biggest hurdles in writing about my relationships. As much as I don't want to blame God or my church for my current state of singlehood and my inability to land a spouse, I do.

There. I said it.

All the songs I sang in church as a child assumed I'd one day have a husband and children of my own. All the lessons I heard as a young woman used the phrasing "When you are married and have a family"—never "If." Even as an adult, from sermons over the pulpit to lessons with other grown women I hear the messages of how important it is to have a strong marriage, to raise good children, and how those two elements of life are more important than any other earthly endeavor. So where does that leave a single woman?

To be fair, my search for a cause is completely irrational. There is no one really to blame. All the platitudes apply here. Just haven't met the right one. Dodged a bullet with this guy or that guy. Timing is everything.

The platitudes don't rub my back when I'm sick. They can't help me decorate a Christmas tree. They can't tell me I'm not a complete failure at life, even when I feel like it. And that is when I know that Cliff Poncier in *Singles* has it all wrong. Even he figures it out. All it took for him was a sneeze.

Toward the end of *Singles*, Cliff tells the audience that he doesn't need anyone in his life after all, and then announces he has to leave, because some pals are waiting for him. It's supposed to make us laugh—he says he is content with being alone, but two seconds later he's off to be with friends. By the end of the film, he sees the woman he spent months leading on, the woman who didn't want to give up on him but eventually did. He pays her a compliment, and a few minutes later, she sneezes. He says, "Bless you," something the woman always wanted in a man. They look at each other, epiphanies in their eyes, and they kiss. He is her Wentworth.

A couple of months after Col. Brandon left, I was talking to Bingley about how I needed to get back to the place where I was okay with being alone.

"Do you really see yourself as being alone?" he asked.

"Well, yeah, of course I am," I said.

"That's interesting, because of all the words I'd ever use to describe you, 'alone' would never even be a consideration," he said.

"Hm. I don't know what to tell you," I said.

But what I really wanted to tell him was this:

I have over 100 contacts in my cell phone, but never feel like I can call anyone. When I'm having a particularly bad day, I definitely don't call anyone. I "handle" it by eating, crying, or ignoring the emotion altogether, hoping it will go away. No one is obligated to listen to me. And I don't want to inconvenience my friends, most of whom are married with children and have way more important things to do than bother with the unimportant problems I have. That doesn't mean I don't find ways to burden my friends just the same.

Stueve is my partner-in-crime at school. He advises the Yearbook and Video Yearbook and teaches video journalism and creative writing. He's about as busy as I am. Plus he writes. All. The. Time. And while he generally respects my choice to not drink, he exerts his peer pressure in other crazy pursuits, like convincing me to do National

Novel Writing Month, or to do a weekly vlog documenting our first year as sponsors of major publications. He has a beard and long hair and an absolutely infectious laugh. The summer that Col. Brandon and I were together, Stueve was my male sounding board. A "man's man," I could share with Stueve things that Col. Brandon said or did and get his perspective on whether this was a relationship worth pursuing.

About a week before Col. Brandon broke up with me, he and I had talked about the coming school year and how it was going to drastically change our time together.

"What will you need from me?" Col. Brandon asked.

"Honestly, I'll just need you to listen," I said.

"Okay . . . now, just to clarify, do you really want me to just listen? Or do you want me to listen, then give you advice?"

I laughed. "Most of the time, just listen. But if I need advice, I'll be sure to specify," I said.

"Okay. I just know that sometimes a woman needs to vent, and other times she needs a little perspective. You just let me know when you need what," he said.

I recounted that exchange to Stueve the next day, in that day's installment of "Do You Think He Likes Me?"

"Uh, when can I meet this guy? I think I want to marry him!" Stueve said.

So it came as no surprise when Stueve saw my swollen eyes and runny nose post-breakup, his first reaction was, "Want me to kick his ass? Sully (a mutual friend) and I will totally hop on our bikes, find him, and beat the crap out of him."

A week later, I sat at my desk picking at my lunch, unable to focus and still weepy. I apologized to Stueve.

"Apologize for what?" he asked.

"It's been a week. I should be over it by now. This is ridiculous," I said, holding back as best I could the sobs that tried to escape my throat.

"Dude. He broke your heart, man," he said. "You don't just get over that in a week."

It was the first time I actually thought of what Col. Brandon did as "breaking my heart." I had used all kinds of other idioms to classify his actions.

He ended it.

Called things off.

Decided I wasn't for him.

But Stueve's word choice suddenly made me realize I could give myself permission to mourn a little longer. It wasn't a meaningless summer fling. Col. Brandon and I had something real, and its end was just as real.

Stueve helped me accept that it's okay for me to fall fast, and it's okay for me to cry when I hit the ground.

# I (Don't) Know What Boys Want

Jane Austen's men seemed to value beauty above all else. Even Mr. Darcy, often considered the ultimate man, declares his love for Elizabeth in an utterly offensive way. After listing all of her faults—including her social status, smarts, sarcastic nature, and inability to withhold her opinion—he resigns himself to the idea that he still loves her. Good Lizzy initially tells Mr. Darcy to beat it, but as we all know, his kindness in saving the family's reputation is endearing, and she changes her mind and decides she loves him too. So what does Mr. Darcy love about Elizabeth?

From my cursory investigation, Elizabeth is so different from other women he has met. Caroline Bingley, who is within his socio-economic class, throws herself at Darcy, but he is unmoved by her advances. Elizabeth is smart, confident, and can hold her own in debates and conversation. I'm also certain that even though Darcy belongs to the ruling class, Elizabeth's open judgment of those with money actually endears her to him.

And let's not forget this trope: the more a woman ignores or shows her disdain for a man, the more desirable she becomes. Oh also, she is beautiful.

So let's break this down a little: Darcy loves Elizabeth because she is intelligent, reads, and has a spicy personality. I have all of these traits. But then the other reason. She's beautiful. In all of my dating years, only two men have told me I'm beautiful. So I'm not sure if I am, really. And self-confident? Well, that depends on where I'm observed. If I'm observed in my school building, I come across as confident. But if I'm out with friends on a Friday night? Not a whole lot of confidence at all. So Austen teaches me that intelligence alone is not enough—I must be gorgeous and confident, too.

What about Anne Elliot, the aging spinster heroine of *Persuasion*? Why does Captain Wentworth love her? I couldn't find as much research about Anne and Wentworth as I could about Elizabeth and Darcy. To be truthful, I'm not sure why he loves her. But the letter he writes her clearly intimates there was something about Anne Elliot that infected Wentworth beyond his own capacity to get over. What always strikes me about this letter is that I identify so much with Anne: she is smart as most Austen heroines are, but she isn't as pretty as she once was.

Even her father admits that her looks will likely prevent her from marrying. But I think Wentworth loves Anne because she loved him when he was poor. She saw what he could become, and even if he didn't become a wealthy and successful naval officer, she would have loved him anyway. I am positive Wentworth loved Anne simply because she believed in him.

I've been there before. With Knightley. And that might be why, out of all the men I've dated, Knightley is the only one who feels to me like the one who got away.

But I've also done this with other men I've dated. I see their potential, and I see where they are when I'm with them, and the love I feel for them outweighs any of the uncertainties brought about by their own insecurities. When I shared that sentiment with Knightley, and 13 years later with Col. Brandon, they each had identical responses.

Though the syntax differed slightly, the upshot was this: "I am not good enough for you. You can do better. And it's not fair of me to expect you to wait for me to become the kind of man worthy of a woman like you."

When Knightley told me this, it launched a three-hour therapy session in the Wasatch mountains that ended our relationship. He had decided he wasn't good enough for me, and rather than fight him on it, I let him go.

Thirteen years later when Col. Brandon gave me the same excuse, I reacted much differently.

"There is only one person who can decide if a man is good enough for me, and that is me," I nearly yelled at him late one night.

"I am just afraid that I'm going to ruin you. And you're so special, so precious," he said.

"Look. If you don't want to be with me, that's a different issue," I said.

"That's not it at all," he said.

"Well then, you need to let me decide what is best for me. You can't make that decision for me," I said.

He reluctantly acknowledged that I had a point. But I wasn't done.

"You're not in an appropriate frame of mind to really

be making these kinds of decisions right now, anyway. And I get what you're saying, I really do. I'm sure you think that trying to let me go came from a place of genuine concern. But I am in this for the long haul. I like you a lot. I care about you more. And I know our situation is complicated, but it clearly hasn't kept us from developing a relationship. You've told me you can be stubborn. I can be stubborn right back when it counts, and this counts. I told you once that I can't imagine anyone not fighting for you. This is what it looks like."

I felt so empowered after that conversation. With Knightley, I rolled over and let him decide. With Col. Brandon, I fought. If he wasn't going to be with me, he needed to give me a different reason . . . which he eventually did. But it wasn't going to be because he thought he wasn't good enough for me. Like Anne, I didn't care about all of his shortcomings. I loved him regardless.

What about the more recent representations of men? Well, it's not that far off from Austen. Blaine likes Andie because she is different, unique, and doesn't let others define her worth (in theory, anyway). Oh, and she's beautiful. Keith likes Amanda Jones because she's beautiful, and ends up loving Watts because Watts is his best friend. Jake Ryan loves Samantha Baker because she's beautiful. Lloyd Dobler loves Diane Court because she is smart, aloof, and beautiful. Diane Court is his Elizabeth Bennet.

I'm not ever going to come close to how these girls are written. And as I navigated the cesspool of online dating, it became clearer to me. Men are looking for very traditional beauty. I'm not that. And I don't know if they want intelligence—they can't get past my looks to find out if my personality and smarts can compensate for my chubbiness and plainness. And the only men who looked at me online were over 50. So to some degree, I'm just as shallow as the men my age. They aren't looking at me because I'm not beautiful, and I'm not looking at 50 year old men because they are old.

# Random Hopeful Encounters

In 2010, I attended the National Council of Teachers of English convention in Orlando, Florida. After a day of invigorating sessions, I graded papers as I sat by the water of our Disney resort. A man approached me and asked if he could sit with me. There were plenty of other seats around, but he wanted to sit with me. And he started to talk to me. Asked me questions about where I lived and what I did and what my teaching philosophy was. And I asked him questions. He ordered dinner, and I picked at a plate of nachos. And we talked and talked and talked, and before I knew it, the sun went down and we had been talking for over three hours.

He wasn't wearing a ring, and even though he appeared much older than what I usually go for, I was so comfortable with him that I didn't care. I wanted him to ask for my email address or phone number. That's his job as the man—Blaine and Duckie both chase Andie, Keith chases Amanda Jones and eventually literally chases Watts, Steve chases Linda. But this man in Florida didn't ask for my email, and now it just lives in my memory as a nice conference encounter. One that I think about often.

He wanted to talk to me. He didn't have to keep

talking to me for as long as he did—he could have made up any number of excuses to bail. But he found me at least interesting enough to be with for three hours. Why can't other men make that same connection? I need an explanation, and I need one soon. Because I fear that even if I lose 40 pounds, grow out my hair and get Botox, I will still be alone.

Cameron Crowe's film *Singles* probably did more for my expectations than any other film. Every main character does end up with someone in Wentworth-like situations. This troubles me, because it is these situations that imbue me with the hope that one day I will open my mailbox or read a text message that will signal Col. Brandon's return.

Even though I am fairly certain that will not happen.

Every year when I teach film genre to my Popular Culture Studies class, I spend a day on Romantic Comedies. We discuss the cultural myths that are perpetuated in Romantic Comedies. It takes them a while, but the kids eventually start to get it. These films teach that love at first sight happens, happens regularly, and is successful. They teach that there is only one suitable mate, and that the whole point of this life is to seek out that one suitable mate.

I've always had a hard time with this idea that there is only one person suitable for my companionship. How debilitating! One person? What are the chances that I'd ever even find him? Out of seven billion people? And what if this one person was a total loser and gave up on finding me and settled for the first bimbo he met at a stupid New Year's Eve dance? Then where does that leave me? Alone forever, because he couldn't be patient or more diligent in finding me? And why does it have to be some sick kind of cosmic treasure hunt in the first place? What if That One Soul is Armenian? How the hell am I going to meet him in Nebraska?

At the same time, though, *Singles* helps me feel a little less hopeless. Each one of the main characters does not want to be alone. Janet, played by Bridget Fonda, admits that, at 23, she thought she'd be married with kids. At 23! This seems so young. She is ever hopeful, though almost to her own demise. Her devotion to her boyfriend, Cliff, is so blind that even when he tells her that he sees other people, she refuses to hear it. He is honest with her, but Janet (like myself, sometimes) would rather have the illusion of a boyfriend than no one at all. And while they do break up during the course of the movie, by the end, they are back together.

Sorry if that was a spoiler for you.

Once again, movie magic reinforces and brainwashes me to believe that one of the men I've dated in the past will resurface at just the right time. He will realize how much he missed me and how perfect I am for him, and we will live happily ever after.

As I rewatched these key films and reread *Persuasion* as prep for this book, now that it's near the end, I can confidently say I'm no longer Duckie. I'm Linda, from *Singles*.

Linda is fiercely independent. Ecstatic to finally have her own space, successful in her career, she still hopes to find love. And when she meets Steve, she fights it, due to a pretty significant prior heartbreak. They have a whirlwind courtship, and after just a few weeks, Linda is pregnant.

(Don't worry Mom, I've never been pregnant. I'm getting to the point quick.)

She expects Steve to bail. Why wouldn't he? He's a guy. This is heavy, real-life stuff. Why stick around? Because he wants to. She fights him on it, claiming it will be too hard, that there's too much baggage involved. But Steve sees through Linda's resistance, and calls her out on the real issue: fear.

And that's it. Right there, that's exactly my problem. It is terrifying to even contemplate that someone might want to be with me despite the extra weight, or the abandonment of my dining room table in favor of my couch, or my 80-hour a week job. Because truthfully, what must be wrong with him if he'd want to take all that on?

So Linda finds her way out—a miscarriage—and assumes that the only reason Steve proposed was because a child was involved. She buries herself in work (as does Steve) and they break up. It's safer for Linda that way, and I completely get it. What Linda does at the end of the movie is a risk I can't seem to take. As the viewer, I know it's completely safe for her to go over to Steve's apartment. She doesn't know that he tried to call. She doesn't know that he is Howard Hughes-ing it in his apartment. She takes the risk. Hope springs eternal. She knocks on his door, and asks to be part of his life again, in any capacity.

Of course, because Cameron Crowe wrote the script, Steve takes her back. It can happen in the movies like that, so why not real life? Because. Nothing in real life is guaranteed. I could drive to Texas tomorrow, show up on Col. Brandon's doorstep, tell him I just want to know him again, and he would probably pick me up, put me back in my car, and tell me to never talk to him again. But there's always a part of me that thinks about taking a page from Linda's book . . . isn't there always a chance he misses me as much as I miss him?

Despite all the heartbreak I've experienced in my life, I'm always surprised at how I still look at the world through my Austen-Hughes-Crowe-colored glasses. Every place I go, I am thinking in the back of my mind, maybe today is the day I find him, or he finds me. We'll have some meet-cute story to tell at parties. The problem is that my insecurities make me dense.

One Friday night, looking particularly haggard, I went grocery shopping. It was the middle of winter, and I was doing my best impression of Ralphie's little brother from *A Christmas Story*. My knee-length puffy coat was still zipped, my scarf and mittens lay in my grocery cart, and who knows what my hair looked like since I took off the knit hat I was wearing. I had just put in a 14-hour day at school and never once retouched my makeup, and since it was Friday, I was exhausted. But I wanted waffles and bacon for breakfast Saturday morning, so I had no choice but to grab a few things (waffles and bacon) before I went home.

I weaved through the grocery store, trying not to make eye contact with anyone in my frazzled state, to my last stop: the bacon aisle. I'm not picky on my source of pork nitrates and usually go for what is cheapest. A man was already standing in front of the selection of bacon offerings, so I stood behind him, surveyed the prices, and grabbed a pound of the cheapest kind. It was the last one.

"Hey, I was going to get that one!" the man said.

He flashed an adorable smile at me.

"Oh. Um. Do you want it?" I said, as I half-heartedly held the bacon toward him, my hollow eyes fleeting up to meet his.

He laughed—not at me, I don't think—and said, "Oh no, you can have it."

"Okay. Thanks," I mumbled, and I hurried off to the checkout stands.

It was then that my brain caught up with the bacon encounter.

Julie, he was hitting on you, my brain said.

No way, said my ego. Have you looked in a mirror? No way he was hitting on you.

You underestimate yourself. I'm pretty sure he was hitting on you, my brain said.

When I told the story to my friend Nikki on Monday, I got as far as the part when he said he wanted the bacon I had picked and she shouted, "He was totally hitting on you!"

"No way," I said.

"Um, guys don't just randomly talk to women in the

grocery store, Julie."

"Whatever," I said.

So I asked two male friends at work. They concurred. I had been hit on in a supermarket, and I didn't even know it. I didn't want to know it, and I didn't want to acknowledge it, because it would have ended in heartbreak. But the hope is there just the same.

Whenever I see a new face at church, a man sitting by himself, even though I know he probably has a wife at home or in another state if he's military, I have seconds or minutes of hope. Maybe he is single. Maybe.

And when he turns out not to be single, I get a little more deflated.

Photo by Ashley Crawford Photography

# I'm Done This Time. Really.

Despite my better judgment, two years post-Col. Brandon, I plunged back into the cesspool of online dating, and a man emailed me. He seemed funny. He wrote in complete sentences with proper grammar and spelling. I enjoyed his emails and felt we were getting to know each other. Then he asked me to meet, and I'm an advocate of meeting sooner rather than later, so we decided on dinner and a movie. Cliché, but it works.

Except when it doesn't.

Except when there's not an ember of chemistry whatsoever.

Except when the conversation is so stunted that at one point the only thing I could think to say was "This is the biggest Panera I've ever been in."

The night before the date, I felt unsettled. This happens often. I need to pay attention to my gut, as it's a fairly reliable warning system. The dates I'm most worked up about end up being train wrecks. The dates I hardly stress over are fantastic.

Anyway, unsettled. So I was, as girls are wont to, dissecting my feelings with my sister and with friends at school, and I said at one point, "I don't want to change my life. I am happy with my space. I don't want to have someone else around."

And I believed it. I felt it in my bones. The thought of sharing my life with another human being was suddenly offensive and unbelievable. People do this? They voluntarily surrender pride and selfishness for another human being? Why on earth would anyone do that?

After I met said squire, what became clear was that I didn't want him around. I do, however, want someone around.

When I started writing this book, the wound from Col. Brandon was still so fresh that I really believed it was a matter of time before we would be back together.

Four years later, we are not.

And despite my horrible luck with online dating, I persisted. I persisted because it is usually safe. I get to banter via email, in the style of Jane Austen, and sometimes we meet and sometimes we don't. I like the emails; they are safe. I get the adrenaline rush of an email appearing in my inbox, and usually, prior to meeting, the emails are flirtatious and sweet. After we meet, I rarely hear from the young squires again. But those emails provide a human connection, an emotional connection I crave.

On the rare occasions the men want to meet me in person, I panic. What will they think of how I look? Doesn't matter if we've had weeks of lighthearted chatter via email or text; I decide before shaking any hands that any relationship will not happen.

After years of falling too fast I turned into someone who wasn't even willing to go anywhere near the ledge. I want to flog myself for the follies of my past, the daydreams of a life with any of my suitors. I think back to how shamelessly I chased Bingley, or even how I tried to fight for Col. Brandon, and that girl embarrasses me. How did I morph into a girl too terrified to even think about falling in love?

I currently have one crush, who doesn't even live within a day's drive. Perhaps that's why it's a crush: distance makes him safe. He doesn't know I exist. Or if he does, he doesn't let me know he knows I exist.

He makes me swoon with a simple status update. His interests mirror mine. His lack of attention to me combined with the elements of his being (LDS, liberal, sports fan, music aficiando, poet, English teacher) have made him irresistible. My behavior and thoughts are juvenile and as such, a tad disturbing. I know part of the intensity I feel is that I see him as The Great White Hope. There can't possibly be someone more suited to me than him. But distance and silence assure me that I'll never really know, so I will wither in unrequited adoration for a season and hope it passes soon.

The act of having a crush is crushing me, and this time I will just let it crush me until I am flat, until I no longer feel, until I am back to looking at couples in a state of supreme awe and marvel, no longer wanting any of it for myself.

Anytime I get a toe-hold on living my life alone—any time I start to feel 100% content with living my life alone, random men wander into my life, often on their way to someone else's, and nearly crush me with hope, with expectations. And because of my LDS upbringing and programming that "God is behind everything," I struggle to believe these encounters are random.

There is a reason these men wander into my life, I'm taught to believe, but at this point it's starting to feel cruel. God is Lucy, holding a football, and I am Charlie Brown, always ready to score a field goal. But just as I approach, that football disappears and I am flat on my back, wondering what happened, then slowly curling into the fetal position and disappearing for a few days. That's been the story now for 22 years, and I cannot do this anymore. I've learned that as narcissistic as I like to be, I have to allow for the possibility that while any of the men I fell in love with might have been great companions for me, I might not have been exactly what they needed. How many of them would have been okay with me working, or writing, or being a Democrat? How many of them instead needed a woman who is content with staying home, happy to choose wifery and mothering over any outside-the-home endeavor?

Perhaps they needed someone who didn't have progressive political or religious views, because those views would have been too much of a challenge for their own sandy paradigms, and the comfort of a parochial approach to religion and politics keeps them centered. Maybe they needed a woman a little more secure in her physical appearance because they weren't going to tell their wives daily that she was beautiful. Maybe they needed better cooks.

The point is, all this time, I've made it about me.

None of the boys wanted me (and that is still true, to some degree). But maybe the deeper meaning is that they needed something different than what I could give. I know on the surface it is little more than mental gymnastics and semantics, but it works.

I started online dating in 1998, because at the time I was impetuous and angry at Knightley for not committing to me. I met a nice man named Clark, and two weeks before Knightley and I finally decided to be an official couple, Clark drove through Omaha on his way to Louisiana and wanted to meet me. He stayed at a Holiday Inn and suggested I meet him in the lobby and I could drive him around Omaha and he would buy me dinner. He was cute enough, and we really clicked on a personality level, but I was so attached to Knightley that I didn't really give Clark a chance.

Maybe I should have.

Maybe if I had allowed myself to feel something, anything, for Clark, I would've saved myself years and years of hope and despair that accompanies online dating.

Because the truth is, I haven't had a serious relationship since Tilney, and every relationship since has been mediated by a computer. It's not normal, and it's not okay. But I'm not meeting people any other way. Here's the problem: online dating since Col. Brandon has become akin to emotional cutting.

I check the online website to see how many men have looked at my profile. And many men have. Few of those men are under the age of 60. The ones who are don't send me messages. And if someone deigns to send me a message and I find him remotely interesting after one week of communicating, my mind goes to some very dangerous places.

I think of whatever holiday is approaching and wonder what it will be like to have someone to celebrate it with.

I think of driving home from school after a long day and calling someone who actually cares how my day was.

I think of cooking dinner and doing dishes in my kitchen and talking to a real live human being about a story from NPR.

I think of falling asleep to the sound of someone's breathing, of reaching across a bed to touch someone's hand, of curling into the side of a companion's body to feel a bit of extra warmth.

Dangerous, dangerous places I go.

And I go there quickly. Too quickly. And if, after a week's time, he has decided to stop emailing me, I am sad—not at the loss of the man, necessarily, because I don't know him well enough to miss him. I miss what he represents.

And I do this over and over and over again. I cut little tiny scrapes across the surface of my heart to remind myself of my capacity to love and adjust my lifestyle to make room for someone else. And it recently dawned on me that this might not be the healthiest of things to do to myself.

After yet another hope-filled encounter, only to

discover that said hope-filler was not officially divorced yet (again...I mean, really, where do I find these men?), I realized that I hate what I become when I have the audacity to hope. I become more critical of my appearance. I live and die by sporadic communication. I feel my eyes hollow out and I ooze loneliness and patheticness from every pore. So, one impulsive Wednesday evening, I deleted every online dating account I had.

For so long, I'd viewed online dating as my offering to God, that I was willing to subject myself to outright horror to find a spouse. But that Wednesday evening, this thought shocked me: what if the real faith is letting go of trying to find someone? What if the real trust in God is trusting that I'm fine and special and valuable as His daughter, regardless of whether a human man agrees? The euphoria of hope reminds me how wonderful it is to feel wanted, how validating it is for someone to hint that I might actually be desirable. But the devastation of reality reminds me of how much happier I am when I am level. When there are no prospects. When I am content with my simple life in my tiny apartment, where I can eat dinner on the couch and fall asleep to a TV show I've seen a million times. My life is mine. I can take a road trip to wherever, whenever, and I don't have to run it past anyone.

(I can block out of my mind the fact that it's incredibly lonely to drive across the country with no one in the passenger seat.)

I know I've declared this in the past, but I really mean

it this time: I have to stop online dating. The emotional toll it takes on me isn't good for my mental health. In the aftermath of a letdown, I just want to sleep, I don't want to work or go to the gym or talk to people. Because sleep is the only place I can escape. These are not normal reactions to an email relationship ending after one week. And I get especially worked up when I can see the men are online but not talking to me.

So in the interest of my own health, it is time that I stopped. When someone engages in destructive, depressive behaviors, the first things that must go are triggers. Online dating has only been a trigger to make me doubt my worth in this world, so it's time to dispose of it.

Maybe that's the actual leap of faith—the faith isn't that God will bring me and a man together via an internet connection.

The faith is that God can do it without one.

# What's God Got To Do With It?

I spend many days fighting the devil that sits on my shoulder. He's loud and obnoxious and tells me I'm ugly and fat and that no one will ever want to be with me. He tells me the reason Knightley bailed is because I wasn't pretty enough. He tells me the reason Tilney bailed is because I was too old. He tells me the reason Col. Brandon bailed is because I was too fat. And he's so convincing, because no one is telling me anything to the contrary. And to top it all off, one day, not long after Col. Brandon had broken my heart, I saw a former student— way chubbier than me, and "pretty in her own way"— walking with her significant other, toting her newborn. She can have a baby. She can find someone to be with her. I should be glad that I didn't have a baby at 19. I don't know what her relationship is like. It could be a total joke. I hope it's not—she's a sweet girl. But when that devil on my shoulder has me comparing myself to every married person around me, it never ends well.

Despite my efforts to wrest away all the blame from God and place it at the feet of Popular Culture, at the end of the day, I do blame God.

I'm so angry at Him sometimes. I imagine He looks at me and every little mistake I make, like cussing and gossiping, and the big mistakes, like shacking up with an abusive jackass for four months, and He decides there isn't enough grace in the world to make me good enough for someone to marry. It doesn't matter how much service I provide, or how much tithing I pay, or how often I try to be a good person. It's as if He looked at me from on high and decided I wasn't ever going to be good enough for one of His sons. Even as I write it, I realize it's ridiculous, but what other explanation is there?

Maybe that's the whole point: I need an explanation. How can everyone I know—my family, my friends, my colleagues—keep telling me how wonderful I am, yet every first date I go on is a bust, or every attempt at a relationship ends in epic failure? I need a reason. I need it to make sense of why I have to be the one to take out the trash and make dinner and do the laundry and have an emotional meltdown completely alone. It's not fair to have to do all of this alone.

I could paint the picture of the woman scorned by many an LDS man yet remains faithful. I could give advice on any of the following:

How I cope with loneliness (best answer: be a friend, actual answer: watch TV)

How I cope with bitterness (best answer: pray, actual answer: list the things I'm able to do, unsaddled by a spouse or children)

How I cope with insensitive comments at church (best answer: smile and nod, actual answer: rant to my sisters)

How I cope with a shrinking dating pool that more

and more resembles Table Number Nine from the film *The Wedding Singer* (best answer: have faith, actual answer: endure random occasional set-ups, and rejections via phone, text, Facebook, etc . . .)

How I cope with not being a mother (best AND actual answer: teach, love my nieces and nephews)

But this is why I can't leave my faith, why I can't leave God: every now and then—fleeting as the moments may be—I don't think of myself as a single person; I can't focus on what I lack. I can only think of what I am, what I do, what I have. Rare, fleeting moments of peace and understanding that I really am okay.

Moments like these don't come easily, and don't usually last too long. But when they do, I feel empowered. These brief moments remind me that my career is valuable—and valued—and not just something to do until I get married. I focus on how much I love being an aunt, and remember how my nieces and nephews clamor for my attention when I'm around.

More importantly, I glimpse how I hope God sees me: not as a "single person in a married church," but as a person working hard at life, trying to fix her mistakes and finding joy in the life she's leading. Because single or married, isn't that all God wants from His children? In these moments of clarity, I am equal to my married, mothering sisters and friends.

And occasionally my Mormon tribe shows me that I belong, because of who I am, not in spite of it. One Sunday my bishop had some extra time so he shared part of a commencement address from a graduation at

BYU. This particular address suggested to the graduates that it was a Christian responsibility to fight marriage equality.

As he spoke, my face flushed and I held back tears. I was so tired of hearing how marriage equality was to blame for weakening marriages. How about forgetting how to date a spouse? How about kindness? Selflessness? Praying together? It's so easy to look outward at society and blame all kinds of external factors for the destruction of marriage, but what's really needed to save "traditional" marriage is some good old-fashioned introspection and suspension of selfish pursuits.

Says the never-married person.

By the time the "Amen" was said, I was sobbing. The woman I sit with every week put her arm around me and asked what was wrong.

"I'm so tired of coming to a place where it's clear I don't belong," I started. "I don't know how much longer I can keep showing up only to hear such awful things, things I don't believe, things I disagree with, things that are flat-out mean."

Then I felt someone sit to my right. It was my bishop.

"Did I do this?" he asked.

"Yes," I said.

The woman to my left got up and walked away, leaving me in the pew with my bishop.

"Is it because you're single?" he asked.

"This has nothing to do with my marital status," I snapped. "It's because you just blamed marriage equality for the divorce rate," I said.

196

I couldn't look at him, afraid I would lose my nerve. I had never been so open with someone about my politics at church. I believe politics should be left out of church, but the 5th grader in me was screaming, "He started it!"

"So many other things contribute to marriages failing. If you were concerned about couples thinking about divorce, don't go after marriage equality. Ask them if they are dating. Ask them if they are praying together. But placing blame on failing marriages at the feet of gays and lesbians is unfair," I said through sobs.

"That was not my intent. I'm so sorry," he said.

I can't remember what he said after that, because I was aware of the time, and I was late to my responsibility of teaching the adult Sunday School class. So I focused on looking for an end to the conversation so I could, like a good Mormon girl, go fulfill my church responsibility.
But my bishop sat with me for ten minutes, he listened to my concerns, he tried as best he could to make sure I knew I belonged in that chapel.

When I arrived in the Sunday School classroom, eyes swollen and makeup looking a tad less fresh than it usually does, another friend—a man whose sons I dated in high school—was standing at the front of the class, ready to teach my lesson.

"Whew. Class is lucky you're here. Glad I don't have to do this after all," he said.

I took a moment to reflect on what had transpired in the last 15 minutes:

I had a complete emotional meltdown.

From 30 feet away, my bishop noticed it and wanted

to make sure I was okay.

While my bishop was listening to my concerns, another person covered my Sunday School class.

My tribe took care of me.

It wasn't the first time people at church have found ways to take care of me, and it probably won't be the last. As often as I feel ostracized as a single person, I also feel valued for what I bring to my congregation. As many times as I feel enraged at misguided but well-meaning comments, I feel enveloped in the arms of Jesus. For every instance I swear I'm never going back, someone tells me she is glad I showed up.

Recording moments like these gives me the opportunity to re-read and remember them when I am feeling lonely, when I am feeling "less-than." In these moments, I am a daughter of God, pure and simple.

That's something that Austen, Hughes, and Crowe can't give me. While they shoulder some of the blame for irrational daydreaming, I find no solace in their texts. But I do, at times, find solace in my faith.

Some Sundays when I'm playing the organ at church, I let my mind drift into Austen territory—that a man walks into the chapel, confesses his feelings for me, and wants to marry me. But that daydream never happens, so I turn to my faith and pray for a momentary epiphany—that I am enough on my own—to last longer than a moment.

# Acknowledgments

This book relied on an army of people to make it possible. First, thank you to AE Stueve for somehow convincing me that writing a book in the middle of an epic heartbreak was a good way to process the pain. I think you may be on to something. Thank you for reading six drafts.

Thank you to all the good folks at EAB Publishing for your feedback and support, and for believing my stories were worth a wider audience. Special thanks to Britt Sullivan for your wise feedback, Madison Larimore and Jeremy Morong for your keen eyes, and Tim Benson for saying yes.

Thank you to Bingley, for your continued support after all these years.

Thank you to Deanne for allowing me to kidney punch her after dating Wickham. That always makes for a good story. And thank you for validating my side of the story. Lylas.

Thank you to the other members of my family for not disowning my boy-crazy self and all the shenanigans that accompany such a personality. Mom, Dad, Jennie, and Brent—I love you.

Thank you to Nikki, Amy, Jenn, Becca, Marya, Adam J. and Andrew J. for helping me hone my storytelling skills. Special thanks to Ashley Crawford for taking photos that made me feel beautiful for the first time since my senior year of high school.

Parts of the chapter "What's God Got To Do With It?" were published at Segullah.org on Aug. 21, 2009. Segullah was the first literary journal to accept any of my personal essay writing, and I am forever grateful for their dedication to nurturing LDS women authors, poets, and artists.

And if I forgot to thank you and you feel you deserved a thanks, then I am sorry and you are welcome to notify me of this omission and I will take you out for ice cream.

Finally, thank you to Wickham, John, Knightley, Tilney, Willoughby, and Col. Brandon. Without you, this book would not exist.

Made in the USA
Lexington, KY
16 December 2015